CONRAD

HEART OF DARKNESS

NOTES

COLES EDITORIAL BOARD

OTABIND

Bound to stay open

Publisher's Note

Otabind (Ota-bind). This book has been bound using the patented Otabind process. You can open this book at any page, gently run your finger down the spine, and the pages will lie flat.

ABOUT COLES NOTES

COLES NOTES have been an indispensible aid to students on five continents since 1948.

COLES NOTES are available for a wide range of individual literary works. Clear, concise explanations and insights are provided along with interesting interpretations and evaluations.

Proper use of COLES NOTES will allow the student to pay greater attention to lectures and spend less time taking notes. This will result in a broader understanding of the work being studied and will free the student for increased participation in discussions.

COLES NOTES are an invaluable aid for review and exam preparation as well as an invitation to explore different interpretive paths.

COLES NOTES are written by experts in their fields. It should be noted that any literary judgement expressed herein is just that — the judgement of one school of thought. Interpretations that diverge from, or totally disagree with any criticism may be equally valid.

COLES NOTES are designed to supplement the text and are not intended as a substitute for reading the text itself. Use of the NOTES will serve not only to clarify the work being studied, but should enhance the reader's enjoyment of the topic.

ISBN 0-7740-3269-3

© COPYRIGHT 1996 AND PUBLISHED BY
COLES PUBLISHING COMPANY
TORONTO—CANADA
PRINTED IN CANADA

Manufactured by Webcom Limited
Cover finish: Webcom's Exclusive **Duracoat**

CONTENTS

Joseph Conrad: Life and Works

Ernest Hemingway once said that "a writer writes about the country he knows, and the country he knows is in his heart." This quotation is especially appropriate to Joseph Conrad because his stories of the sea, the jungle, the social and political instability of mankind and the innermost workings of the human heart are commentaries on and reflections of his own life and varied experiences.

For example, *The Secret Sharer* deals with a situation similar to a much publicized incident which occurred on the *Cutty Sark*, and *Heart of Darkness* is linked with the months Conrad spent in the Congo. These works, however, must be regarded as more than autobiographical, for Conrad did not hesitate to rearrange times, events and characters.

Just as Conrad's story lines were drawn from experience, so were many of his characters. Captain John McWhirr of the real ship, the *Highland Forest*, appears under his own name in the novel, *Typhoon*. Marlow's aunt in *Heart of Darkness* is drawn from Conrad's real aunt, Madame Marguerite Poradowska, and, Antonia De Avellanos, in *Nostromo*, is patterned after Conrad's childhood sweetheart, Tekla Syroczynska.

The Early Years

Joseph Conrad, christened Jozef Teodor Konrad Nalecz Korzeniowski, was born to Polish parents at Berdichev in the Russian Ukraine on December 3, 1857. His father, Apollo, had married Evelina Bobrowska, the daughter of a well-to-do family of landowners who were not overly fond of their temperamental son-in-law, who was known to the Czarist police as an agitator. Apollo was certainly devoted to Polish independence although, in later life, Conrad insisted his father could not rightly be termed a revolutionist. Conrad called him "simply a patriot in the sense of a man who, believing in the spirituality of a national existence, could not bear to see that spirit enslaved."

But the police considered Apollo dangerous and in October, 1861, arrested him for engaging in activities against the Russian government. Along with his wife and young son, Apollo was shipped to the prison camp at Vologda, in northern Russia, for four years of exile. Camp life was too hard for

Evelina and, in 1865, she died of tuberculosis, leaving Jozef with his despondent father. His own health damaged by his imprisonment, Apollo was subsequently released, at which time he and Jozef returned home.

Apollo was forced to educate his son as best he could. A man of letters, he had for years translated French and English literature into Polish. Young Jozef's first acquaintance with the sea came from reading the galley proofs of his father's translation of Victor Hugo's *The Toilers of the Sea*. Similarly, Jozef's introduction to Shakespeare and other noted English authors was the result of further readings of translated manuscripts.

However, Apollo began to show the effects of his difficult imprisonment which robbed him of the strength to care for his son. In 1869, Apollo died of tuberculosis, and young Jozef became the ward of his uncle, Tadeusz Bobrowski.

Over the next twenty years Jozef and his uncle became like father and son. Tadeusz saw that the boy attended school in Cracow and gave him both love and comfort. But Jozef was dissatisfied with school; it was too regimented, too boring for his passionate, romantic nature. He wanted to go to sea, but he rejected an opportunity to attend the Austrian Naval Academy in Pola.

He spent the summer of 1873 in Switzerland and northern Italy and, on a trip to Venice, he had his first glimpse of the sea. When he returned to Poland, he resided for a short while at Lwow where he fell in love with his cousin, Tekla Syroczynska. But his thoughts went outward—toward Western Europe and the sea—and, in 1874, he departed for Marseilles and 20 years of naval adventures.

The Adventurous Years

Jozef arrived in Marseilles with an annual allowance of two thousand francs. Employed by Delestang and Sons, bankers and shippers, he served an apprenticeship aboard the *Mont-Blanc* on her voyage from Marseilles to Martinique and then to Le Havre. Back in Marseilles, he signed on the schooner *Saint-Antoine* for a voyage to the West Indies, in July, 1876.

At this time Don Carlos VII, Bourbon claimant to the throne of Spain, was making his bid for a kingdom. Marseilles was the center for Carlist intrigue and Conrad found himself involved in it. In 1877, he purchased a share in a sailing vessel, the *Tremolino*, and smuggled arms to the Carlist supporters. Before long, however, Conrad and his partners were forced to destroy the *Tremolino* to prevent its falling into enemy hands and Jozef lost his investment. At about the same time, he had a short-lived and unhappy love affair. Dejected and deep in debt, Conrad apparently attempted suicide. Uncle Tadeusz arrived in Marseilles, paid Jozef's debts and saw him through his convalescence.

His experiences in France having proved somewhat unsatisfactory, Jozef turned his attention to the British navy. He signed aboard the British vessel, the *Mavis*, and sailed to Constantinople. In June, 1878, the *Mavis* returned to its home port and brought Conrad for the first time to England where he had no friends and did not know the language.

Only fragments of the facts of Conrad's life during the next ten years are known. Through diligent efforts he overcame the language barrier and mastered the art of speaking and writing English. He received his third-mate papers in 1880, his first-mate papers in 1883 and his master's papers in 1886. Also in 1886, Conrad became a British subject and first tried his hand at writing—a not very good short story, unsuccessfully submitted to a fiction contest.

Conrad was becoming less and less content with his life at sea. He was not only injured several times in accidents aboard ship, but he was also filled with a growing sense of tedium. Out of this boredom, in 1889, he began writing a novel, *Almayer's Folly*. Also, as a result of boredom with the now familiar sea routes, he became obsessed with the idea of Africa. Perhaps his desire to go to Africa was prompted by a map in some Fleet Street window, perhaps it was the recurrence of a boyhood dream. Whatever the reason, Conrad was determined to secure work as a captain on one of the steamers plying the snakelike Congo River. His aunt, Marguerite Poradowska, who lived in Brussels, was instrumental in getting him the appointment he wanted. In April, 1980, Conrad sailed for Africa. This experience is clearly the basis for much of *Heart of Darkness*.

A year later, Conrad returned to England where, weakened by gout and malaria, he managed a Thames-side warehouse for a year. During his shore duty, Conrad continued to work on his novel, *Almayer's Folly*. From late in 1891 through 1893, Conrad was again on the sea. Early in 1894 he was back in London and his naval career had come to an end.

The Literary Years

Conrad's finished novel, *Almayer's Folly*—its central figure patterned after the Dutch trader, Olmeijer—was, at the urging of Conrad's friends, submitted to the publisher, Fisher Unwin. Unwin's reader, Edward Garnett, who was to become one of Conrad's staunchest champions, was immediately impressed by the book and persuaded his employer to accept it. It came off the press in late 1894 when Garnett insisted that Conrad begin another immediately. He rather reluctantly gave in, and found himself launched on the literary career that was to bring him increasing fame, the most intense creative agony and, eventually, a measure of affluence.

Thereafter, the notable events in Conrad's life became, with very few exceptions, the content and the essence of the books he wrote. His second novel, *An Outcast of the Islands*—another story of a man's degeneration in the tropics—involved Lingard, Almayer and other characters from Conrad's first novel, and appeared in March, 1896. A week later, Conrad married an English girl, Jessie George, whom he had met a little over two years earlier. They honeymooned for a few weeks in Brittany, where Conrad worked on some short stories and suffered a violent attack of the arthritic ailment that incapacitated him regularly for the rest of his life. He also began work on a third East Indian novel, *The Rescuer*, of which Tom Lingard was to be the hero. This book gave him such trouble that he eventually put it aside and did not return to it for many years. Frustrated, he turned to the sea, ships and seamen of his own experience. He wrote the first of his great sea pieces, *The Nigger of the "Narcissus,"* which was first published as a serial, then as a book, in 1897. The next year a collection of short stories, *Tales of Unrest* was published. Most of the stories are minor works, but *The Lagoon* is admired, and *An Outpost of Progress* is an interesting sketch on the same theme as *Heart of Darkness*. *Tales of Unrest* marks the end of Conrad's formative period, in which most of the works are clearly the experiments of a talented amateur. *The Nigger of the "Narcissus"* alone compares with the works of the mature Conrad, but it, too, contains some obvious inconsistencies.

In 1898, Jessie gave birth to the Conrads' first son, Borys. Their second son, John, was born eight years later. Though Conrad was now known by his pen name, both boys were christened Korzeniowski. To add to the family's cares, Jessie had fallen in 1903, injuring her knees so badly that she remained a cripple, despite a long series of operations. On the brighter side, they developed a growing group of friends and acquaintances, including such writers as Stephen Crane, Arnold Bennett, H.G. Wells, Hugh Walpole and Ford Madox Ford.

In late 1898, Conrad first met the twenty-four-year-old Ford, whose original name was Hueffer. Ford, too, was a budding author and a cockily self-confident young man. For reasons that are not clear, Conrad suggested they collaborate. The results were: (1) *The Inheritors* (1906), a trivial flight of fancy written mostly by Ford; (2) *Romance* (1903), a shallow but exciting adventure story which was a genuine collaboration and which somewhat foreshadows *Nostromo*, and (3) *The Nature of a Crime*, which Conrad disclaimed entirely.

The next decade saw an almost continuous outpouring of books, most of which form the body of Conrad's greatest work. In 1902, two of the very best, *Youth* and *Heart of Darkness*, together with a lesser novella, *The End of the Tether*, were published in book form as *Youth: A Narrative and Two Other Stories*. While it was being serialized, the manuscript of the last half of *Tether* was burned and Conrad had to rewrite it from memory. A somewhat inferior collection, whose title story nevertheless ranks among Conrad's masterpieces, was *Typhoon and Other Stories* published in 1903. *Nostromo* (1904), an epic study of the effect of power and wealth on human minds in a South American republic, had its origin in a glimpse Conrad had had of the Venezuelan coast on one of the early West Indian voyages. For the next several months he turned out more stories, some articles and worked on *Chance*, which he temporarily abandoned in 1906. That same year, he published a volume of autobiographical sketches called *The Mirror of the Sea*. The ironic *The Secret Agent* was published in 1907 and, in 1908, *A Set of Six*, a collection of rather trivial short stories.

A long siege of bad health and family troubles slowed the writer down. It was not until 1911 that *Under Western Eyes*, his "Russian" novel, still so pertinent to the world situation today, was published. Another volume of personal retrospection, *Some Reminiscences* (now called *A Personal Record*), came out in 1912, as did a fifth book of short stories, *'Twixt Land and Sea*, notable chiefly for *The Secret Sharer*. *Chance* came out in 1913.

In 1914, the Conrads visited Poland and became trapped by the outbreak of World War I. Only by devious methods were they able to return to England five months later. The experience left Conrad depressed and exhausted. Nevertheless, he was able to bring out *Victory* (whose title he found ironic under the circumstances) and still another group of short stories, *Within the Tides*, in 1915. Though the reviewers had always praised his books, he did not catch on with the public until the publication of *Chance*. Now, as his powers began to decline, his popularity and his sales went up. *Victory* was a smashing success. He published *The Shadow-Line*, perhaps his last great work, in 1916. At this time, he brooded over his son, Borys, who had joined the army, and then served a brief tour of active duty with the Royal Navy. In 1919, came *The Arrow of Gold*, the theme of which he had tried and abandoned more than twenty years before in a fragment now called *The Sisters*. In 1920, *The Rescuer* (retitled *The Rescue*) was at last finished. Three years later Conrad produced his final completed novel, *The Rover*, a tale of post-revolutionary France.

Shortly thereafter, at the invitation of his American publisher, F.N. Doubleday, he visited the United States. He then set to work on another, more ambitious, historical novel, *Suspense*. But his health began to fail badly and, on August 3, 1924, while sitting alone in his room, he died of a heart attack. After his death, the uncompleted novel was published, as was a miscellany of previously uncollected short stories under the title, *Tales of Hearsay*. There also exist two volumes of essays (*Notes on Life and Letters* and *Last Essays*), a large number of variously collected letters and three plays, all drawn from his stories.

It is sufficiently remarkable that a middle-aged man of action with little formal education should produce a novel; it is more so that the novel should be published. Even more astonishing is the fact that such a man, starting at an age when many people are coming to the end of their careers, should have turned out fourteen novels and eight volumes of tales, the least of which invited comparison with the best being written by most of his contemporaries. As if this were not enough, one must recall that Conrad, born to another tongue and untrained in the grammar and syntax of any, established himself as one of the great stylists of the English language. Most astounding of all is that this sickly, moody, self-doubting Polish sailor should have done so much to revolutionize the whole concept of prose fiction.

Conrad's Ideas on Life and Art

Conrad believed that the world rested on "a few very simple ideas; so simple that they must be as old as the hills." He believed that the most notable of those ideas was what he termed "fidelity." His concept of the word is implied in Marlow's comment about the Roman commander in primitive England: "Oh, yes—he did it [his duty]. Did it very well, too, no doubt, and without thinking much about it either, except afterwards to brag about what he had gone through in his time, perhaps." Conrad believed that every man should do his duty, an attitude he developed through long experience on ships at sea, where, if a man shirked his duty, all might be lost.

To Conrad, life could be meaningful only through work that produced an understanding of mankind's common destiny. He further believed that work was man's shield against evil, for through work man could prevail and could forge the ideals needed to overcome the darkness.

In a period of revolutionary literature, Conrad refused to be revolutionary. Here, again, his feelings were solidified by his career at sea. His conviction that it was the spirit of service, not the spirit of adventure, that was important guided his work, and he desired to present ideas, not to attract attention. To Conrad, love of adventure was "no saving grace," and he mistrusted the mere soldier of fortune. Conrad did not doubt that the soldier of fortune had courage, but he believed that it was a worthless kind of courage because it lacked the steadying influence of an underlying ideal.

The adventurer was not a worker, for he had nothing to work toward. Without guidelines, the adventurer was really a soul adrift; he might cut and run in any direction at any moment. He was under no sense of restraint and he lacked the "steady fidelity" that Conrad felt was mankind's saving grace.

Like Poe, Conrad believed that "a work that aspires, however humbly, to the condition of art should carry its justification in every line." Upon a first reading, however, many of his stories appear to deviate from this axiom, particularly when the reader struggles through some of the descriptive passages. On closer examination, one finds that Conrad remains true to his dictates, for even the wordier passages perform an artistic function. Certainly, in *Heart of Darkness* Conrad is interested in mood. His settings advance and intensify the mood. Through such intensification, Conrad hopes to create a "sinister resonance, a tonality" that will envelop the reader long after Marlow's tale is finished.

To Conrad, the artist was one who sought the truth in the world of ideas. Unlike the scientist, the artist did not deal with facts and, therefore, could not appeal to the reader's common sense or intelligence. Instead, the artist must seek out that part of human nature which is hidden behind the mask of the ego and make his appeal to the more basic qualities of humanity. Conrad based much of his appeal on archetypal patterns or motifs. One such motif is the quest in which the hero must go on a long and dangerous journey. He must perform impossible tasks, battle monsters, solve difficult riddles and overcome terrible obstacles in order to attain his goal. A second such motif is the initiation in which the hero must undergo a series of ordeals while passing from ignorance and immaturity to social and spiritual adulthood. This initiation usually consists of three stages: separation, transformation and return.

For fiction to be successful as art it must, in Conrad's opinion, appeal to the senses—sight, smell, sound, touch, taste. This theory accounts for the impressionistic effects of Conrad's narratives. In Conrad's own words, "My task which I am trying to achieve is, by the power of the written word, to make you hear, to make you feel—it is, before all, to make you *see*. That—and no more, and it is everything."

For Conrad the aim of art was to capture one moment of life and freeze it, so that mankind might pause and see such a moment for the truth it contained. If the writer could successfully freeze this moment, one could see that "all the truth of life was there." Such accomplishment is no easy matter. The artist's intention is to create an entire world in which he can believe, and such a world must necessarily be fashioned from his own conception of life. Since each man is different, there is a danger that the world of the artist may seem strange. Therefore, one last task stands between the artist and his goal. He must make his world plausible as well.

The difficulty of this is compounded by the fact that the artist deals in symbols. Conrad believed that a work of art could seldom be so limited that only one interpretation was possible. In fact, the nearer "it approached art, the more it acquired a symbolic character." Though this symbolic character might give added depth and power to the work, it also increases its complexity. When combined with Conrad's deliberate use of implication, this symbolic approach can blur a reader's sense of familiarity with the world created in the novel. That readers did have difficulty is shown by the many different critical evaluations of Conrad's work.

To Conrad, literature was of no more importance than any other distinct form of action. It annoyed him that many writers felt they were superior beings with some kind of special task. For Conrad, there was no more justification for literature than for "any other artistic achievement. In the sum of human effort it [has] no special importance." If the artist has any advantage over other individuals, it resides in his privilege to think freely and the opportunity to express his innermost philosophies. For the writer of fiction Conrad recommended humility, faith and the recognition that, although the world is not necessarily good, there is no "impossibility of its being made so."

Conrad's Technique

Like Conrad's ideas, his method is too complex to allow a detailed treatment in so short a space, but certain general characteristics can be outlined here. Perhaps the most obvious of them lies in the organization of the stories themselves. Each work usually presents or implies a pattern to which men, for better or worse, may commit themselves in the hope of living in relative harmony. Outside that pattern stand certain individuals ("isolatoes" as one critic has called them) who try, or are somehow forced, to live independently of it. The chief dramatic tension is generated in the conflict between society and the isolato. A simple example is provided by the renegade, Willems, of *An Outcast of the Islands* who, out of desire for a native girl, betrays the benevolent Lingard and so opens to anarchy the peaceful world the latter has built at Sambir. Two opposite poles are provided in *The Nigger of the "Narcissus"* by the active Donkin, who offers the crew a hope of better things through mutiny, and the passive, dying James Wait, who tempts them with the escape of apathy. The thick-headed Captain MacWhirr of *Typhoon* is a less obvious example. Unable to imagine a tropical storm, he ignores the pattern provided by the navigation books and, taking the shortest course to his destination, sails right through one. He does so out of fidelity to his mission, and he saves the ship through fidelity to duty. But, in the process, he dimly discerns that there are higher laws that make individual wishes and plans ridiculous or pitiful. Opposed to the isolatoes and the experimenters are such types as the dogged, old sailor of the *Narcissus*, Singleton, and the steersman of the *Nan-Shan*, who come through by doing what they must.

In Conrad's so-called political novels, the device is necessarily more complex. In *Under Western Eyes*, for example, the desirable pattern exists only by implication in the relationships between individual characters. Razumov, for all the loftiness of his motives, is a deliberate loner. Conrad obviously has no sympathy with either the czarist tyranny or the revolutionaries. In *Nostromo*, the brilliant and cynical Decoud is clearly an outsider, and the Montero brothers and their followers provide an equally clear image of anarchy. But the admirable Charles Gould and Nostromo himself, along with most of the other "good" characters, are betrayed by circumstances and their own shortsightedness into isolation from the rest of humanity and, inevitably, into the destruction of their lives and spirits.

One could multiply such examples endlessly, for they provide the gears that move the stories. Building a piece of machinery is one thing; making it function successfully is another. It is generally in the point of view from which the stories are told and in the handling of sequences of events that Conrad makes the machinery function successfully.

One understands one's environment through the impact that sensory reactions have on the mind. All art is properly sensuous—aesthetic rather than intellectual—and it is through the appeal to the senses that Conrad makes his approach. He reports carefully and objectively on what one would hear, feel and see about his subjects; he does not intellectualize. Rarely, when Conrad is narrating, does one see, hear or feel more than if one were present at the scene. But Conrad does call the reader's attention to those things that he *must* see to understand.

In order not to interpret for the reader, Conrad, as narrator, avoids commenting on his own reactions to the dialogue, action or situation. Yet, in highly complex stories like *Chance*, it would be unfair to ask the reader to make his way wholly unaided. So, rather than narrating the story himself, Conrad adopts the device of having the story told by a character in it—such as Marlow, who narrates *Heart of Darkness*. One is able to know, understand and empathize with Marlow to the same degree that one does with any other fictional character. One understands his strengths and weaknesses and his particular approach to life. One recognizes him as garrulous, as cynical, as a man of ideals who has painfully learned the truth about idealism. Thus, when Marlow offers opinions or speculates about the thoughts or motives of other characters, the reader does not feel he is being manipulated by the author. Instead, he has a sense of hearing a story told by an acquaintance and can evaluate the opinions and speculations in accordance with his knowledge of the narrator-character. Conrad does not always use a narrator. He tells some stories in the third person, as objective a viewpoint as possible, as in *The Rover*. In others— *The Secret Agent*, for example—the mood is more subjective. In still others, such as *Nostromo*, though no narrator is specified, it is apparent that Conrad is assuming a Marlowlike mask to tell the tale.

A third device that Conrad uses to emphasize his meaning is the "time-shift" or "working back and forth" technique. Here, he works, not with chronological time, but with so-called human time. In actuality, events progress through time but that is not always the way people experience them. In order to grasp the significance of any given episode, our minds are constantly reaching back into the past and forward into the future in an attempt to discover meaningful relationships. It is this process that Conrad tries to duplicate, forcing the reader's mind to go through the same sort of movement it would if he were actually involved in the experience. In trying to make sense of Lord Jim's life, for example, the narrator moves back and forth, one episode reminding him of another, until the whole seemingly random and chaotic pattern is drawn together into a logical web.

Related to the time-shift technique is one that has been described as "cinematic"—in the manner of a motion picture. This method allows the reader to move about, to look at things from a distance or close up or even superimposed on one another. He is not forced to see things from a fixed position and at a fixed distance, as in stage plays and older novels. Thus, as the writer Edward Crankshaw points out in the first pages of *Nostromo*, we look at the Gulf from the town and at the mountains from the Gulf; we walk through the streets noting faces in the crowd; we are carried for a moment by some reminder into the past; we stop to examine the surrounding details. We assimilate a wealth of information, seemingly random and casual but, actually, carefully planned by the author to lead to a comprehension of the whole structure of the novel.

It is such careful planning that brings us to a final, important aspect of Conrad's literary method and, perhaps, the most subtle: that the techniques of poetry are applicable to prose fiction. Poetry produces the maximum effect in the smallest space by letting *every* aspect of the poem—words, meter, rhyme, form, and so on—contribute to what is being said. Similarly, Conrad saw—and preached—the need for making every detail, every happening, every fluctuation of sentence rhythm, every choice of image and word, however minor, essential to the meaning of the whole. One cannot avoid noticing in *Heart of Darkness* the crucial interplay of words and phrases dealing with white and black, light and dark, good and evil—pairings in which one antithetical term seems to turn into its opposite, under the reader's eyes, thereby underlining the central paradox of two "successful" modes of human existence that corrupt each other upon contact.

Conrad's Influence and Reputation

Something remains to be said about Conrad's place in literature. Despite the acclaim he won throughout his writing career and the popularity he enjoyed in his last years, it is doubtful whether most readers and critics, during his lifetime and for some years thereafter, had any real notion of his importance. He was far ahead of his time and, though the critics wrote appreciatively of his exciting plots and vivid descriptions, they regularly missed his central excellences. There were some, however, who saw his true worth. They were chiefly young writers—mostly Americans—of the post-World War I generation, who were seeking a way to present the chaos of the world. Among them were Scott Fitzgerald (*The Great Gatsby* provides a stunning parallel to *Heart of Darkness*), William Faulkner and Ernest Hemingway. It would be safe to say that Conrad's influence on fiction, particularly on American fiction, has been incalculable.

The professional critics really began to notice Conrad in the 1930s. In 1936, Edward Crankshaw's *Joseph Conrad: Some Aspects of the Art of the Novel* was published, a brilliant and penetrating study that is basic, not only to an understanding of Conrad but, also, to an understanding of contemporary literature. In 1940, John Dozier Gordan published *Joseph Conrad: The Making of a Novelist*, a painstakingly detailed study of the sources and composition of the earlier works. A year later, Muriel C. Bradbrook's little study, *Joseph Conrad: Poland's English Genius*, won considerable attention. What some scholars regard as "the Conrad industry" began to flourish. Since World War II, many excellent books and articles have appeared, including those by F.R. Leavis, Albert J. Guerard, Thomas C. Moser, Leo Gurko and Eloise Knapp Hay.

Introduction to *Heart of Darkness*

Heart of Darkness is the artistic projection of Conrad's personal journey to the Congo in 1890. Although Conrad's life before this was characterized by sea voyages and miscellaneous adventures, there is no doubt that the Congo journey was the prime influence that determined Conrad, the sailor, to become Conrad, the novelist. For Conrad, the expedition to the Congo became a journey within, a journey through darkness into the self.

While much of the biographical information of Conrad's journey is available from letters and remembered conversations old friends had had with the writer, the singularly interesting and most important source is the diary kept by Joseph Conrad. The "Congo Diary," as it is commonly called, is composed of two small, black, penny notebooks, written in pencil. One of the notebooks is initialled, J.C.K.—Joseph Conrad Korzeniowski. The first entry is dated 13 June, 1890. In the second notebook, dates are, for the most part, omitted, and it is impossible to discover when the final entry was made. Moreover, place names are lacking while they are used extensively in the first. Though it is certain that the diary was begun while Conrad was at Matadi (the Company station about one hundred miles above the mouth of the Congo River), it is impossible to say where it was ended.

We know from "A Personal Record" that Conrad reached the area of Stanley Falls, "The farthest point of navigation." Furthermore, it is in this same book that we learn how, as a little boy in Poland, Conrad had announced that he would go to the center of Africa.

In *Heart of Darkness*, this same audacity is displayed by Marlow, who, looking at a map of the Congo in a bookseller's window in Fleet Street, is reminded of these same childhood desires.

In 1889, the Congo was of universal interest. Since 1875, various economic speculations and exploratory expeditions in Africa (the most famous being Stanley's from Zanzibar to the Lower Congo in 1876 and 1877) had aroused in Europe the most ardent interest and the most violent greed.

Brussels, where Conrad went to seek a contract as a riverboat captain, had become a hive of activity. It was the chief city for embarkation for what Stanley had called the "Dark Continent." Adventurers, missionaries, men of good will and rogues met there with their varied motives—faith, greed, violence and simple curiosity. It is no wonder that this atmosphere of adventure and discovery stimulated Conrad and intensified his urge to command one of the wretched little steamboats of the Upper Congo. The trading company needed a captain who could speak French, and Conrad met this requirement perfectly. The Company was new and was expanding considerably. Nevertheless, while it needed new men, Conrad had to wait several months before he finally found himself aboard a ship, the *Ville de Raceio*, bound for the Congo. The ship took thirty-four days to reach Boma, the station nearest the mouth of the Congo. From there he went to Matadi in a little steamboat. His work was not to commence until he reached Stanley Pool, some two hundred and fifty miles upriver.

Conrad soon became aware of the risks involved in this adventure, although they had certainly not been explained honestly in Brussels before his departure. In a letter to his cousin, Charles Zagérski, he stated:

> . . . I have been told that 60% of the Company's employees go back to Europe, without even staying six months . . . others are hastily sent back after a year so that they won't die in the Congo. Heaven forbid! That would spoil the statistics, which are excellent, you see! In brief, it seems that only 7% can stand three years service . . .

From the first, Conrad was disillusioned and his attitude toward people he met was one of detachment:

> Think just now that my life amongst the people [white] around here cannot be very comfortable. Intend to avoid acquaintances as much as possible. (Congo Diary)

This remark begins the first notebook of Conrad's "Congo Diary" which he kept in English from June 13 to August 1, 1890, the period of his stay at Matadi and the long trek from Matadi to Kinchassa.

While waiting to begin his overland journey up the Congo, Conrad spent his time as best he could in activities that had little to do with his proper vocation. He writes, "Have been busy packing ivory in casks. Idiotic employment." The same day he also notes: "Prominent characteristic of social life here: people speaking ill of each other." The atmosphere of this colonial outpost certainly did not appeal to him.

At last, on June 28, with a caravan of 31 porters, he left Matadi with Prosper Harou, an agent of the Company who had been Conrad's travelling companion all the way from Bordeaux and who seems to have been constantly ill, needing to be carried most of the way. The country that Conrad travelled through was unpleasant. After a week of marching over rocky terrain in scorching sun, camping at night in the damp and cold, bad water, mosquitoes, porters' threats of mutiny, Conrad comments in his diary: "getting jolly well sick of this fun." Finally, after nine days, the expedition arrived at Kinchassa, the home port of the Upper Congo flotilla. There the Company had set up a kind of shipyard where ships were assembled or repaired.

In Kinchassa, Conrad contacted Camille Delcommune, temporary acting manager, who becomes "the manager" in *Heart of Darkness*. In a mood which is increasingly cynical, Conrad gives these first-hand impressions in his dairy:

> My days here are dreary. There is no doubt about it. I decidedly regret having come here; indeed, I regret it bitterly. Everything here repels me. Men and things, but especially men. And I repel them, too. From the manager in Africa—who has taken the trouble of telling a lot of people that he can't stand me, down to the lowest mechanic—they all have the gift of getting on my nerves.
>
> The manager is a common ivory-dealer with sordid instincts, who considers himself a trader when he is nothing but a kind of African shopkeeper. His name is Delcommune. He hates English, and, of course, I am regarded here as an Englishman.

It is fairly certain that the manager, Delcommune, prevented Conrad from obtaining the command of the *Florida*, the ship he was to have originally captained, as an effort to keep Conrad a subordinate. It is obvious that the manager became the principal cause of Conrad's discontent.

On the same day that he arrived in Kinchassa, Conrad

17

embarked as second officer on a steamboat, the *Roi des Belges*, and, the next day, continued up the Congo River. Captain Koch, a Dane who had been upriver several times, instructed him about the dangers and difficulties of fresh-water navigation.

Twenty-eight days after her departure, the *Roi des Belges* arrived at her destination, Stanley Falls. This voyage, which, by the standard of the day, was considered extremely fast, must have seemed interminable to Conrad for, in *Heart of Darkness*, it attains the length of "just two months."

It was during this trip that Conrad received the impressions that became the essence of the *Heart of Darkness*—the sense of solitude, which was not only a result of his being "in the heart of an immense darkness," but also because of the fact that he no longer felt any rapport or solidarity between himself and his European companions. He no longer felt that common bond of human dignity, that fidelity to simple, yet civilized, moral principles which, during his childhood and his fifteen years at sea, had been honored as a safeguard for an ideal code of human conduct.

The purpose of the voyage of the *Roi des Belges* was to retrieve one of the Company's agents at Stanley Falls. This agent, whose health was failing, and whom Conrad later transformed into the terrifying figure of Kurtz, actually had a similar name, Georges-Antoine Klein. He had arrived in the Congo late in 1883 and was placed in command of the Company station at Stanley Falls in 1890. He died on September 21, aboard the *Roi des Belges*, and was buried at Bolobo, not far from Kinchassa, by the steamship's company.

The exact relationship between Kurtz and Klein is not certain but, when one considers that Conrad was in the habit of employing in his works elements drawn from reality, these two figures, one actual, the other fictitious, are found to be similar in more than just name.

It was during this time that Conrad's health was seriously impaired and, by October 19, he had decided to give up everything and return to Europe. He had held out as long as he could. He was defeated as much by human malice as by the effects of the climate. Ironically, Delcommune's ill will toward Conrad must be regarded as good fortune. If Conrad had been given command of the steamship, it is unlikely that he would have returned from the Congo alive.

The immediate result of this journey to the Congo was, in Conrad's own words, "a long, long illness and a very dismal convalescence." He never regained his health. He suffered from attacks of fever and gout for the rest of his life. On the other hand, this voyage and its deplorable consequences did become the most decisive factor in his becoming a novelist. Joseph Conrad had once told his friend, Edward Garnett: "Before the Congo, I was just a mere animal," meaning that he experienced in Africa a peculiarly intense insight into the possibilities of evil in man. His most direct testimony of this vision is his story, *Heart of Darkness*.

Superficially, *Heart of Darkness* consists of three, fairly long divisions or chapters, labelled by Conrad merely I, II and III. More subtly, however, the novella may be regarded as a complex and dramatic structure, complete with prologue and epilogue. Each of the three parts comprises some half-dozen separate yet closely interwoven scenes of varying length, all dramatically and naturally linked.

A close scenic analysis should enable the reader to see the author at work planning and stage-managing the larger lines— the framework—of his story and, with great finesse, fitting his narrative bits and pieces together into scenes that, starting from the prologue, swell slowly and rhythmically toward Marlow's climactic confrontation with Kurtz. Thus, Conrad the artist is ever conscious of the necessity of making the structure of his story support his artistic aim, linking that structure to subject and theme.

Needless to say, except for the Roman numerals that mark the chapter divisions we have termed "Parts," nowhere does Conrad allow his novelistic or dramatic seams to show to any extent, so subtly does he weave scene to scene and chapter to chapter. For purposes of clarification, chapters and scenes have been titled to describe their content and their place in the narrative or dramatic flow of events. Reading the Summaries and Commentaries allows the reader to follow the narrative flow of events in Conrad's story, as well as to better appreciate his strong structural and dramatic support of those events. It must be emphasized that the following titles were not affixed by Conrad, but for the purpose, here, of clarifying the basic dramatic structure of the plot. Each of Conrad's larger divisions has been subdivided into scenes.

Plot Summary

Part I

The novel opens at sunset on the deck of a cruising yawl, the *Nellie*, which is at anchor on the Thames. Five men are lying back to rest and meditate, waiting for the tide to turn. One of them, Charles Marlow, thinks aloud about ancient England at the time when the conquering Romans came seeking wealth and power. He pauses, and then begins to tell of a trip to the Congo he made as a young man. First, he describes how he came to make the trip. Out of a job and fascinated by Africa for a long time, he enlisted the help of an influential aunt who was able to secure him a position as a river steamboat captain. Marlow then goes on to tell the story that Conrad himself had experienced in his own life.

After being examined by a doctor who measures his skull and cautions him to remain "calm" in the jungle, Marlow takes a French steamer to the mouth of the Congo River. The steamer moves very slowly, making many stops along its way, and Marlow marvels at the vastness and mystery of the jungle. They pass a French gunboat firing shells into the dense, black depths of the jungle. Marlow is told that there are enemy natives hidden there, but is struck by the absurdity of this war with the "darkness" and its invisible forces. Finally, the steamer reaches the mouth of the Congo and Marlow disembarks.

Here, he boards another steamer, commanded by a Swede, and starts on the first leg of his journey up the river. The captain tells him of the sad fate of another Swede, who had apparently hanged himself. Again and again Marlow is struck by the incongruity of the European presence in Africa.

Marlow goes ashore at the Company station, which is surrounded by broken machinery, dying slaves, and an aura of useless effort. The company accountant, an oddly out-of-place fellow dressed in a starched shirt, polished shoes and a suit, tells Marlow about Kurtz. It is the first time we hear Kurtz's name; the accountant refers to him, ambiguously, as a "very remarkable person."

Marlow continues his journey into the heart of darkness, trekking through the jungle accompanied by 60 natives and one other white man. He is struck by the wild chaos of the jungle. The group comes upon the body of a native, shot through the forehead. Marlow's European companion becomes feverish and unable to walk. All the native villages they come to are abandoned. The paths are overgrown; the surroundings desolate and terrifying. Finally, after fifteen days of walking through the jungle, they come to the central station.

There, Marlow meets the Company manager who does not even invite him to sit down but, instead, confronts him with another obstacle. The steamer which Marlow was to command has sunk to the bottom of the river. Not only must Marlow raise the steamer and repair its bottom, but he must do it without the benefit of the proper equipment: there are no rivets to be had upstream.

As it happens, it is three months before the ship is repaired and Marlow can start on the next leg of his journey. During his stay, we see several more examples of the madness and inefficiency of European life in Africa. A shed mysteriously bursts into flame one night. One of the Company employees tries pitifully to extinguish the flames using one bucket—which has a hole in it—to carry water from the river. Part I ends at this point with the arrival of the motley Eldorado Exploring Expedition, bound on a mission of greed.

Part II

Part II opens with Marlow on the deck of the little riverboat at the central station. As he lies on the deck, the manager strolls by with his uncle, who leads the Eldorado Exploring Expedition. Unaware of Marlow's presence, they begin to discuss Kurtz with a mixture of dislike and envy. They comment on his moralizing, his courage, and his enormous success in the ivory trade. They also note the high mortality rate among white agents in the jungle. The conversation ends abruptly when they realize Marlow is on the deck listening to them.

The riverboat is finally repaired and a group of pilgrims (Company employees), led by the manager, begins the trip up the river to Kurtz's inner station. The trip takes two months. Marlow is the pilot and his crew consists of a group of twenty cannibals. As the boat progresses up the river, Marlow, impressed by the primitive nature of the country, feels he is travelling back in time. The journey is difficult and his time is taken up trying to avoid the snags and rocks in the river. The pressure takes its toll on Marlow and he begins to feel disoriented. He feels he is being watched by a sinister, brooding presence. As the boat goes deeper and deeper into the jungle, Marlow begins to identify with the groups of natives sighted on shore. He senses a humanity in their savagery and a savagery in the white people with whom he travels.

Fifty miles from Kurtz's station, Marlow and the pilgrims discover a ruined hut where there is firewood waiting for them. There is also a note warning them to proceed with caution and haste. While investigating, Marlow finds a book, *An Inquiry into Some Points of Seamanship*. With this new mystery puzzling him, Marlow guides his little riverboat into the innermost "heart of darkness."

Two days later, eight miles from the inner station and Kurtz, they are forced to anchor for the night because of fog. They are awakened in the morning by a loud, horrible, anguished cry—first one voice, then many—they can see nothing, as they are still enveloped in a thick, white fog. Terror strikes the party. Only Marlow remains calm, convinced that the natives will not attack. As it turns out, he is right and the boat sails on with the lifting of the fog.

Only a mile and a half from their destination they come across an island in the river. To pass the island it is necessary to choose a channel which takes the boat very close to shore, close enough to brush against bushes on the bank. Suddenly, the natives attack. Thousands of arrows fly through the air, and the poleman is the first to duck for cover. Marlow's helmsman is hit by a spear and dies in silence in a pool of blood. At this point, Marlow sounds the boat's whistle and the terrified natives scatter. Marlow wonders if Kurtz is dead.

Marlow pushes the helmsman's body overboard, much to the disappointment of the cannibals, continues upstream, the trading post soon coming into view. Standing on shore is a white man, beckoning to them. He is dressed like a harlequin (a sort of clown) in a suit that has been patched with many brightly colored rags. Marlow discovers that it was this man who left the wood for them down the river and that the book was his as well.

Part III

The harlequin describes his precarious relationship with Kurtz. He has known him for two years and, when Kurtz fell ill, it was he who nursed him back to health. Marlow hears of

Kurtz's ivory raids, and of his mysterious power over the natives. Kurtz is adored; as a result, there is nothing to restrain him from doing whatever he wants, even to killing. Now, however, Kurtz is again ill, and the harlequin pleads with Marlow to take him quickly away from the village.

As Marlow surveys Kurtz's house he notices that the fence posts surrounding it are topped with human skulls. Suddenly, Kurtz appears, carried on a stretcher. Marlow describes him as being very tall and emaciated; his head is bald and white as ivory. The crowd of natives parts in awe as he comes. Marlow gives Kurtz the letters he has brought and retires to the deck of the boat with the harlequin. They both watch in fascination as a magnificent native woman appears.

The manager and Kurtz have an argument about Kurtz's "unsound methods" and, almost in spite of himself, Marlow finds himself on Kurtz's side. The harlequin informs Marlow that it was Kurtz who ordered the attack on the riverboat, and worries about the effect of this on Kurtz's reputation. The harlequin then disappears into the jungle after borrowing some shoes and English tobacco.

Marlow awakens at midnight to discover that Kurtz has disappeared. He experiences a deep "moral shock" but does not sound an alarm. Instead, he goes off into the jungle, alone, in search of Kurtz. On the bank of the river he finds a wide trail. Ahead, Kurtz, too weak to walk, is crawling on all fours. Marlow circles ahead of Kurtz and confronts him only a few feet from a native fire. He reasons with Kurtz, telling him that he will be utterly lost if he does not return to the riverboat. In the ensuing argument, Marlow sees that Kurtz himself is rational, but that his "soul" is "mad." Marlow wins the argument and helps Kurtz back to the boat.

The next day, Kurtz and Marlow prepare to leave. As the boat gets under way the natives gather on shore, but when Marlow blows the whistle they all rush off into the jungle. Only the beautiful, native woman remains.

Kurtz and Marlow talk as the journey continues. Kurtz tells Marlow of his grandiose plans for the future and of the woman he had planned to marry, his Intended.

One night, while the boat is stopped for repairs, Kurtz begins to feel that he is going to die. Close to death, Kurtz goes through a hideous transformation, as if a "veil had been rent."

Kurtz dies after uttering his final words, "The horror! The horror!" The pilgrims bury Kurtz.

Marlow himself becomes very ill and, still physically and spiritually shaky, he goes back to Brussels with Kurtz's papers and the knowledge of his reputation. He finds out a great deal more about the man Kurtz had been from a Company employee and from Kurtz's cousin. He goes to see Kurtz's Intended, and finds her devoted to the illusion that Kurtz was a great and good man. When she questions Marlow about Kurtz's final words, he cannot bring himself to tell her the truth, telling her instead that Kurtz died uttering her name.

The setting returns to the deck of the *Nellie*, and Marlow's story ends with him sitting silently in the "pose of a meditating Buddha."

Characters in the Novel

THE FIRST NARRATOR: He is the fifth man on board the *Nellie*. He serves to introduce the other men aboard, particularly Marlow, who is to be the main narrator. During the course of the story, Conrad takes us back to him just as each part of the novel is ending. He becomes a connecting point for the reader, mirroring the effect Marlow's tale has on the reader. As he moves from innocence to some knowledge of the nature of man, so does the reader.

CHARLES MARLOW: Superficially, he is a man of action, an adventurous sailor. But he is not typical. He is a seeker of truth, one who looks for the deeper meanings behind his experiences. He is dedicated to the British concept of civilization and behavior: doing one's job well, sticking to the track and being faithful.

THE KNITTING WOMEN: One fat and one slim, they are symbolic guardians of darkness. They act as Company representatives. They seem to know all about Marlow. He senses "unconcerned wisdom," like that of the Fates, in their eyes.

THE CLERK: A shabby, young fellow who works for the Company, he wears his hat over his left eye and has inkstains on his sleeves. He goes for a friendly drink with Marlow and glorifies the Company's business, but has no interest in going to Africa. He helps to build up the tension surrounding Marlow's trip.

THE COMPANY DOCTOR: An unshaven, little man in threadbare clothing, he is thought by Marlow to be a "harmless old fool." He is interested in Marlow for "the sake of science" and measures his skull. He hints that Marlow will be a changed man when, and if, he returns. He suggests that the changes will take place *inside* Marlow's skull.

FRESLEVEN: He is the ex-riverboat captain who is replaced by Marlow. He had viciously attacked an old, tribal chief and had been killed by the chief's son. He represents (for Marlow) the bizarre effects the jungle can have on one's sanity.

MARLOW'S AUNT: She is instrumental in giving Marlow the opportunity to voyage into the "heart of darkness." She is representative of all women who, because they are "out of touch with the truth," must be protected from it.

THE SWEDISH CAPTAIN: He commands the vessel that delivers Marlow to the outer station. He is morose, young and lean. He has contempt for the government traders and agents living ashore but is interested in what happens to those who go into the inner regions.

THE ACCOUNTANT: He does his job "properly," and keeps his books in "apple-pie order." He is one of the few Company administrators who commands Marlow's respect, although Marlow senses the madness of his single-minded discipline. It is he who first mentions Kurtz.

THE COMPANY MANAGER: As manager of the central station, he had "managed" to survive the oppressions of the jungle because of his coarse spirit and strong constitution. He is depicted as essentially a hollow man, jealous of Kurtz's success, and very suspicious of his humanitarianism. His machinelike personality is a counterpoint for Kurtz's wild idealism.

THE PILGRIMS: Avaricious employees of the Company, they remain anonymous as individuals. They make their "pilgrimage" to the interior for the sole purpose of exploitation. Capable of murder, they are awful perversions of the colonial spirit.

THE BRICKMAKER: This man lives a pointless existence—there is not one brick at the station. He is ruled by the petty evils of greed and envy, and conspires with the manager against Kurtz. He tries to ingratiate himself with Marlow.

THE MANAGER'S BOY: As if to reflect the character of his owner, the "overfed young Negro from the coast" is shrewish and insolent. It is he who announces that Kurtz is dead. It is indicative of Conrad's artistry that he would make so minor a character deliver such important news—"Mistah Kurtz—he dead."

THE FOREMAN: A boiler-maker and a good worker, he is one of the few people at the central station whom Marlow likes. He is a widower with six children whom he has left in his sister's care. He has a passion for pigeon flying. He is as anxious as Marlow for the rivets to arrive so that he can work.

THE MANAGER'S UNCLE: Aptly described as "a butcher in a poor neighborhood," he leads the Eldorado Exploring Expedition. His physical person mirrors his essence: paunchy and dull-eyed. He seems to serve to foreshadow

Kurtz's death when he points his flipper-like arm to the jungle and says, "Ah! my boy, trust to this—I say, trust to this."

THE HELMSMAN: This swaggering, unstable fellow is scarcely able to steer the riverboat. He dies at Marlow's feet, with his blood filling Marlow's shoes. Marlow admits of a certain kinship with him, but feels that he has "no restraint," paying for his lack of control with his life.

THE HARLEQUIN: He serves an important role in the build-up to meeting Kurtz. Deliberately conceived as a clownish romantic, the harlequin is an ideal convert to Kurtz's doomed illusions.

MR. KURTZ: The epitome of Western European civilization, he enters the wilderness with the progressive idea of uplifting the savages. Instead, he responds to the primitive assault of the jungle with an unsuspected primitivism of his own. Although he is hollow at the core, he is able to realize the significance of his experience and of what he has become.

KURTZ'S JUNGLE MISTRESS: A surrealistic figure, she appears only twice. Conrad never fills in the relationship between her and Kurtz. In her fantastic and rich clothing she is more of a statue than a woman. She is thoroughly devoted to her "white god."

THE INTENDED: The civilized antithesis to the savage woman, she is devoted to the memory of a highly idealized Kurtz.

THE COMPANY REPRESENTATIVE: He is a clean-shaven man who presses Marlow for Kurtz's documents. Marlow refuses to give Kurtz's papers to this walking symbol of the Company's greed.

KURTZ'S COUSIN: A refined person and talented organist, he gives Marlow more information about the man that Kurtz had been. Marlow gives him some letters and memoranda.

THE JOURNALIST: This character is a bristly haired fellow who has followed Kurtz's career and is interested in his fate. He tells Marlow that Kurtz was a charismatic leader, a genius who should have been in politics. He leaves with Kurtz's "famous report."

Summaries and Commentaries

Part I: Into the Heart of Darkness

SCENE I
Prologue

Summary

It is evening on the Thames. On board the *Nellie*, a cruising yawl at anchor and waiting for the turn of the tide, are five old friends, linked by "the bond of the sea:" the director of companies, "our captain and our host;" a lawyer, "the best of old fellows;" an accountant, "toying architecturally" with a box of dominoes; Marlow, sitting "cross-legged right aft;" and the first narrator, the "I" of the opening paragraph and of the last sentence of the story. Each of at least four of the "old fellows" is in a characteristic pose: the director looking seaward; the accountant playing at dominoes; the lawyer relaxed on a rug. All, especially Marlow, who sits cross-legged like an idol, are in a meditative mood as the sun sinks low, "as if about to go out." The first narrator evokes "the great spirit of the past," as well as some of history's storied seamen like Sir Francis Drake—"knights-errant of the sea," who had "gone out on that stream," the Thames, in search of gold or fame.

As if in answer to the first narrator's thoughts, Marlow muses aloud: "And this also has been one of the dark places of the earth." He paints a word picture "of very old times, when the Romans first came here, nineteen hundred years ago," depicting the "darkness" that was then Britain and the "cold, fog, tempests, disease, exile, and death" that the Romans encountered as they "faced the darkness . . . the incomprehensible . . . the detestable." In his Buddha pose, Marlow preaches the creed that he and his listeners respect, the saving grace of "efficiency—the devotion to efficiency," condemning the Romans for being merely conquerors and grabbing what they could. Here, Marlow strongly suggests that the only redeeming feature of that sort of plunder is the "idea at the back of it; not a sentimental pretence but an idea . . . something you can get up and bow down before, and offer a sacrifice to." A long silence follows and the five companions aboard the *Nellie* wait patiently for the tide to turn. It is at this point that Marlow begins his story. "I suppose you fellows remember I did once turn fresh-water sailor," he says. They are fated, the first narrator guesses, "to hear about one of Marlow's inconclusive experiences."

Commentary

The tone of this introductory scene is one of calm contemplation, suggested by the physical setting of the *Nellie* at anchor in the "benign immensity of untamed light" on the Thames at sunset; by the restful and contemplative attitudes of the five men aboard—especially Marlow who is presented as severely introspective; by the historically ranging soliloquies of the first narrator and Marlow about the past (lending to the tale which follows a valid universality); and, perhaps most of all, by Conrad's use of slow-paced, prose rhythms which are partly based on the repetition of such terms as "tranquil," "immensity," "gloom," "haze," etc.

When Scene 1 ends, like the four auditors on the *Nellie*, all are ready to listen to Marlow's tale.

Dramatic Structure: Dramatically, this scene consists of three subtly interwoven subscenes:

(a) The first narrator's introduction of the four other men on the *Nellie* and his description of the sunset on the Thames.

(b) The first narrator's evocation of the past and his list of ships and sailors, "Knights-errant" and "bearers of a spark from the sacred fire."

(c) Marlow's soliloquy on the coming of the first Romans to Britain "nineteen hundred years ago."

Setting: Note that Marlow's story is told aboard the ship, *Nellie*—appropriately suggestive of one of the main symbols of the book: Marlow's archetypal voyage of discovery. The *Nellie* is anchored on the Thames, "an interminable waterway" like the Congo River, the "snake" that tempts Marlow, in his Adam-like innocence, to the journey that leads to self-knowledge.

Note too, that the *Nellie* is at anchor, at rest—just as are its guests, the five men linked by the "bond of the sea." Again, we are told that it is flood-time, the time most symbolically opportune for the voyage Marlow will take. Marlow's Buddhalike lotus posture serves to accent this deeply introspective atmosphere of contemplation.

29

The first narrator informs us that they are waiting for the "turn of the tide." The time of day is dusk, between light and darkness, again symbolically meaningful. The story is filled with these recurring, contrasting images. Marlow proceeds into the heart of darkness to find the light of illumination.

Point of View: When, at the end of this prologue, we read that the four listeners are "fated to hear about one of Marlow's inconclusive experiences," we realize that *Heart of Darkness* is a "frame" story, a story within a story. That is, Marlow's recital is boxed in between the opening and closing words of the novella, which are spoken by the "I" whom we term the first narrator.

Conrad assigns to both the first narrator and to Marlow the first person viewpoint. But the first narrator is peripheral to Marlow's yarn, in spite of the belief on the part of some critics that he is Conrad himself, while the second "I" is the central character, Marlow.

Imagery of Light and Dark: Images of light and dark are used in the prologue as well as in the rest of the story, gaining symbolic value by their frequent use. In Scene 1, the "luminous space" of sea and sky "welded together," the "luminous estuary," the "benign immensity of unstained light," the "august light of abiding memories" and the "stir of lights" all contrast with the "brooding gloom."

The description of the setting given by the first narrator serves, to a degree, to characterize him as having a "lightened," perhaps naïvely optimistic viewpoint (though he is aware of the gloom also). Symbolically, too, light signifies civilization, enlightenment, knowledge and realization. By contrast, the forest is dark. But what seems dark may be light, and what seems light—or white—may be dark. The portrait painted of Kurtz is of a torchbearer, an ironic comment on the dark evil he practises. These examples can be multiplied. What is important is to recognize the symbolic value of the many references to light and dark. Generally, it may be suggested that their recurrent juxtaposition suggests Conrad's theme of the exploration of the shadow—the dark jungle of the unknown—of which the physical journey is a symbol.

Marlow's Soliloquy: Marlow's soliloquy on the Romans illustrates one of Conrad's favorite artistic devices—the miniature foreshadowing of events. Marlow's ruminations about the early Roman colonizers of Britain are, perhaps, in ironic juxtaposition to the first narrator's previous soliloquy with its rather naïve, romantic view of history. Marlow considers Roman exploration and colonization to be full of "disgust [and] hate." This soliloquy foreshadows the modern counterpart of Roman colonization, namely the exploitation of the Congo.

Marlow's Buddha Postures: Marlow is twice described as resembling an idol, seemingly Buddha, near the beginning of the story, once near the middle, and again in the final paragraph. Conrad is suggesting that Marlow has a mission to preach, in meditative calm, the meaning of his descent into the "heart of darkness" where he confronted Kurtz, symbolic of the evil that lurks in Marlow, as in every man.

The first narrator describes Marlow as having "sunken cheeks, a yellow complexion, a straight back, an ascetic aspect, and, with arms dropped, the palms of hands outwards," resembling an idol assuming the meditative position. He is ready to delve deeply into himself, ready to "recollect in tranquility," so to speak. This attitude of modification of the flesh seems to be juxtaposed to the flabby attitudes of the others on board. (Only the first narrator, who is describing this scene, seems aware of the distinction between Marlow and the director, lawyer and accountant.) In short, Marlow's spirituality contrasts with the materialism of the other three.

The total impression in this first scene is that Marlow, in his recital, will again go through every step of his journey to Kurtz, will again vicariously relive Kurtz's descent into evil, will, once more, go through the ordeal of looking into himself. Marlow will descend into his own hell, an arduous exercise.

At the end of Marlow's story he is seen sitting in the lotus posture ". . . apart, indistinct and silent, in the pose of the meditating Buddha." He is now completely detached, purged by the reliving of his introspective descent into the self.

SCENE 2

Preparations for the Voyage

Summary

Prefacing his tale with the modest disclaimer, "I don't want to bother you much with what happened to me personally," Marlow very methodically announces that his listeners, in order to understand his experience fully, will want to know "how [he] got out there, what [he] saw, how [he] went up that river [never named but, clearly, the Congo] to . . . where [he] first met that poor chap"—Kurtz. That place, Marlow tells his audience was the "farthest point of navigation . . . the culminating point" of his experience, an experience that threw "a kind of light on everything about [him]."

Thus, Marlow begins his story by first focussing on his climactic meeting with Kurtz and hinting at the revelatory character and meaning of his adventure, a revelation or "epiphany" that we, as readers, must experience as well. It is only then—after this brief glimpse ahead—that Marlow reverts to chronological narrative sequence.

Marlow had just returned to London "after a lot of Indian Ocean, Pacific, China Seas . . . a regular dose of the East—six years or so," and, feeling restless, began casting about for a ship, a fruitless search of which he soon tired.

When Marlow was young he had had "a passion for maps." "When I grow up I will go there," the young Marlow would say, putting his finger on one of the "particularly inviting" blank spaces on the world map. One of the biggest blank spaces on the map, ". . . through which ran a mighty big river . . . resembling an immense snake uncoiled," was still mysterious to most people. This river—the unnamed Congo—fascinated him, "as a snake would a bird—a silly little bird." It charmed him, in fact, into applying for a job with a company trading in that "place of darkness."

With the help of a doting aunt, "determined to make no end of fuss" to get Marlow an appointment as skipper of one of the Company's riverboats, his opportunity comes when one of the Company captains is killed in a scuffle with the natives. It is only months later, says Marlow, getting ahead of himself again, that he learned the details of this tragic event. It seems that this captain—Fresleven, a Dane—originally "the gentlest, quietest creature," after being "engaged two years in the noble cause . . ." feels the need to assert himself. Thinking himself wronged in a transaction involving two black hens, Fresleven goes ashore to "whack" an old native chief "mercilessly." It is then that the chief's son spears Fresleven to death, leaving his body to rot amid the grasses that eventually grow up through his ribs.

Shuttling back again to a chronological sequence, Marlow

describes his flying around "like mad" to get ready for his trip. Within two days he crossed the English Channel to sign his contract, at Company headquarters in a city—Brussels, presumably—which reminds him of a "whited sepulchre." The Company offices are situated in a narrow, deserted street with grass sprouting between the stones. The staircase he mounts is "as arid as a desert." In an outer office, Marlow meets two women, one fat, the other slim, both knitting black wool. Without a word, the slim woman escorts him into a waiting room where he notices a large multicolored map. He is glad to see "a vast amount" of red, indicating British possession, "because . . . real work" is done there, he thinks. As for him, he is "going into the yellow"—where the river is, dead center, "fascinating—deadly—like a snake."

He is beckoned inside a "sanctuary" by a secretary who has a "pitying expression." Here, behind a desk sits a man of "pale plumpness in a frock-coat," the "great man" in control of "ever so many millions," the Company executive. In seconds Marlow finds his business transacted and himself out in the waiting room again with the secretary. As he signs the necessary documents, he begins to feel uneasy. He senses something "ominous" in the atmosphere. In the outer room the women knit their black wool "feverishly." The old one, whose quick glance seems full of an "unconcerned wisdom," has a cat on her lap. It all seems "eerie and fateful" to Marlow, as if the women are "guarding the door of Darkness."

Now Marlow prepares to go through his medical. Since it is too early for the doctor, he has a vermouth with a shabby-looking clerk who, developing "a vein of joviality . . . glorifies the Company's business." But, when Marlow wonders why the clerk himself has not gone "out there"—to the Congo—the latter replies that he is "not such a fool as he looks."

The old doctor finally arrives and examines Marlow, asking eagerly to be allowed to examine Marlow's head carefully noting its measurements. He explains that it is all in the interests of science to "measure the crania of those going out there," adding that he never sees them return and that changes occur "inside, you know." The doctor then asks whether there is any insanity in Marlow's family, a question which Marlow finds irritating. As they part, the doctor advises Marlow to avoid irritation, to "keep calm."

A final duty remains for Marlow before setting out. He

33

must say good-bye to his "excellent" aunt, whom he finds "triumphant" because of Marlow's success in securing the position she had helped to obtain. In the course of a long chat with her, Marlow discovers that he has been represented by his aunt in glowing terms as an "exceptional . . . creature . . . one of the Workers . . . an emissary of light . . . a lower sort of apostle." At this point in the narrative, Marlow comments on how out of touch with truth women are living "in a world of their own," an unreal world "too beautiful altogether . . ." After Marlow leaves his aunt, he experiences a "queer feeling . . . as though . . . [he] were about to set off for the centre of the earth."

Commentary

Dramatic and Time Structure: This second scene offers an illustration of Conrad's use of time-shift, the technique of working backward and forward in time that Conrad and his collaborator-friend, Ford Madox Ford, devised. Their purpose, so well shown in *Heart of Darkness*, was to make the novel (which, in the past had followed a chronological line) more psychologically true, more complex, more dramatic and more involved, so that the reader would have to consider the novelist's artfully juxtaposed elements of past, present and future in order to discover the chronology of events.

To illustrate: Marlow begins by flashing ahead to tell us that he first met "that chap"—Kurtz—at the "farthest point of navigation." In other words, Marlow gives us a glimpse of the end of the story at its beginning.

Marlow then returns us to the past in London. Immediately, however, he offers us a brief flashback to what he had been doing for six years prior to his arrival in London: sailing the Indian Ocean, the Pacific and the China Seas. He swings back to London again to inform us of his search for a job. But, an instant later, we are again shifted back in time to hear about his boyhood passion for maps and his ambition to explore the blank spaces on them.

Again, in the story of Fresleven, Marlow swings from present to past to future. While Marlow is hunting for a job (present), the Company learns of Fresleven's death (past). It is only afterward (future) that he learns how and why Fresleven died.

Conrad's time-shift technique involves six major steps:

1) careful selection of detail to give the effect of the passing of time;
2) indirect and interrupted handling of interviews and dialogues to give a sense of complexity;
3) parallelling and opposing situations to provide time conflicts and tensions;
4) introducing a character, then working backward and forward over his past;
5) use of a "gathered-up" summary;
6) use of specific time to suggest real life.

Conrad was working toward what we now call the cinematic viewpoint, based on the modern concept that psychological time is different from a chronological succession of lived moments. Past, present and future are all fused in the mind. Thus, the artist should be free to flash back or ahead to reveal past or future, just as the mind does.

The Story's Depth of Meaning: In this scene, when Marlow flashes ahead to his climactic meeting with Kurtz, he describes it as "the culminating point of my experience, the furthest point of navigation." Thus, subtly, Conrad equates Marlow's outward and actual trip up the Congo with Marlow's inner, spiritual journey of self-discovery. By now, the reader will grasp that Conrad—through Marlow—always works from an outer, luminous periphery of images toward an inner, central, symbolic meaning. That is why the first narrator in Scene 1 describes Marlow this way: ". . . to him [Marlow] the meaning of an episode was not inside like a kernel but outside, enveloping the tale which brought it out only as a glow brings out a haze . . . ." More and more now, the astute reader will begin to see the outer facts of Marlow's trip as having inner symbolic significance.

For instance, note what Marlow says about his stay in London. He says, "[I was] hindering you fellows just as though I had got a heavenly mission to civilize you." Immediately, we connect this statement of Marlow's with the first observer's description of him in the previous scene as a Buddha, a religious seer whose mission it really is to try to civilize his listeners. We must see beneath the seeming self-deprecatory and ironic surface of Marlow's statement to the truth beneath it. It is

Marlow's mission to convert his listeners to greater self-knowledge.

Fresleven's Story: This is a story full of ominous foreshadowings and symbolic overtones. That Fresleven was engaged in the "noble" enterprise makes him a blood brother to Kurtz, who also started out as an idealist. But, in the jungle, both Fresleven and Kurtz undergo radical changes. Just as Kurtz gives way to "unspeakable rites," so the originally mild Fresleven gives way to a need for "self-assertion" to the point of "whacking" a native chief in a quarrel over two black hens. The jungle, symbolically the testing ground of man's inner strength, corrupts them both.

The black hens sound a foreboding note, reminding us of the two women in Brussels who knit Marlow's fate in black wool, just as the two black hens settle Fresleven's fate. The association of Fresleven's bones rotting in the grass with the grass "sprouting between the stones" at the Company headquarters is a parallel with symbolic meaning. Bones and grass keep recurring as images that gather resonance as we read. The images of grass—a symbol of life—seem always to be growing amid images of death.

The "Whited Sepulchre": This metaphor is applied to Brussels, the location of the headquarters of the ivory-trading company that employs Marlow. The source of this image is Christ's indictment of the Pharisees in Matthew, 23. 27-28:

> Woe unto you, scribes and Pharisees, hypocrites! For ye are like unto whited sepulchres, which indeed appear beautiful outward, but are within full of dead men's bones, and uncleanness. Even so, ye also outwardly appear righteous unto men, but within ye are full of hypocrisy and iniquity.

The powerful image of the whited sepulchre entombing dead men's bones is an obvious reference to the theme of economic exploitation in that it castigates the trading company—a band of modern Christian "pilgrims"—as a group of contemptible hypocrites who, in the "vile scramble for loot," leave death and desolation in their wake.

It also reminds us that the seeming order, beauty and civilization of a modern city, like Brussels or London, can cloak the same "darkness" that Marlow confronts in the jungle.

36

At the Company Headquarters: Conrad makes it obvious that he is writing on a symbolic level. The colors on the map illustrate this: red is associated with Britain and the work motif; yellow, the color of old ivory, is symbolic of the Kurtzian corruption in the "heart of darkness," the "dead centre" of the jungle, the mysterious darkness in the heart of man. The two knitting women represent the mythical guardians of the doors to Hell into which Marlow descends.

Irony: Marlow's description of his farewell visit to his aunt is an excellent example of Conrad's use of irony. Marlow finds his aunt "triumphant." The irony lies in the aunt's thinking of Marlow's effort in overblown terms. To her, Marlow is not simply going out to do a job. He will be one of the "Workers"—an "emissary of light—like a lower apostle." A "commonplace" affair is how Marlow describes his journey, adding, "I felt as though instead of going to the centre of a continent, I were about to set off for the centre of the earth." In calling such a trip "commonplace," Marlow is ironic, for the "centre of the earth" symbolizes the center of the self, the center of reality and truth, the center of the hell inhabited by Kurtz.

SCENE 3

Along the Coast

Summary

Marlow leaves in a slow-moving French steamer, whose sole purpose seems to be to land soldiers and custom officers at "every blamed port." He watches the coast slip by, fascinated and puzzled by its enigmatic appearance. The sun is "fierce," as they pound along for the absurd purpose of landing clerks to levy taxes in a seemingly "God-forsaken wilderness," and soldiers, presumably "to take care of the custom-house clerks . . . ." It all seems a monstrous farce as they proceed along the coast which always looks the same, "as though we had not moved." They pass places with names like Little Popo, names that seem "to belong to some sordid farce acted out in front of a sinister back-cloth."

As a passenger, Marlow feels a sense of idleness, a sense of isolation and the pressure of the sombre landscape—all producing the effect of a "mournful and senseless delusion," and seeming to keep him "from the truth of things." In this nightmarish atmosphere, the sound of the sea—a natural sound—provides meaning and pleasure, "like the speech of a brother." Similarly, the occasional sight of a boat "paddled by black fellows" arouses Marlow to a "momentary contact with reality," making him feel that he still belongs to "a world of straightforward facts." This momentary feeling of comfort vanishes, however, erased by some incident such as their coming upon a man-of-war anchored off a desolate coast and "[incomprehensibly] . . . shelling the beach . . . firing into a continent." As Marlow puts it, it all seems an insane enterprise, though he is earnestly assured by someone that there is a camp of natives—supposedly enemies—on shore.

Mail is delivered to the man-of-war, on which three men a day are dying. They proceed along the coast, encountering more places where "the merry dance of death and trade" goes on. Nature seems to "writhe" at them in "impotent despair" at their intrusion. Particular impressions become blurred, since nowhere do they stop for long. But Marlow forms a general impression: it is "like a weary pilgrimage amongst hints for nightmares."

After thirty days, they reach the "mouth of the big river"—the Congo. Marlow transfers to the sea-going steamer that will take him upstream. His first stop will be the outer station, thirty miles up the river. The captain of the steamer is a young Swede who expresses bitter contempt for the "government chaps" on shore who will do anything "for a few francs a month." (It is significant that we are left to imagine what that "anything" means. Plunder of the natives seems to be suggested.) The Swede wonders what becomes of "that kind" of official when he goes up country. When Marlow replies that he hopes to see for himself, the Swedish captain tells him about another of his passengers—another Swede—who had hanged himself on a similar trip up the river. "Why?" cries Marlow. "Perhaps it was the sun or the country," offers the Swede, sardonically.

At length, they sight a rocky cliff near which are "mounds of turned-up earth," houses and a "waste of excavations." Amid the constant noise of the rapids and the blinding sunlight, people, "mostly black," move about "like ants." A jetty projects into the river. Three "barrack-like structures" overlook the scene. This is the Company station.

Commentary

This short scene describing the first leg of Marlow's journey, adds to the tone of heartless rapacity and nightmarish absurdity already encountered in the previous scene. The "merry dance of death and trade" is Marlow's description of the greed that he sees. The "farcical" names of the "trading places" passed by the little steamer illustrate the absurdity of European commerce forcefully superimposed on native Africa, as does the "firing into a continent."

Conrad has subtly arranged his first three scenes. The prologue is calm and contemplative; Scene 2 offers a contrasting flurry of excitement and a seesawing back and forth in time; in Scene 3 we travel in one direction, staring fixedly at the passing landscape.

Marlow calls the coast an "enigma" that whispers to him to "come and find out." Interpreting *Heart of Darkness* as a symbolic journey of self-discovery, the enigma of the coast is, in reality, to be equated with the enigmatic human heart. The forest whisper then becomes the compulsive urge within Marlow's being to "come and find out," to undertake the journey within.

In this scene, Conrad emphasizes the absurdity of the attempt of the whites to tame the vast continent. This is illustrated by Marlow's account of the landing of custom clerks in the "god-forsaken wilderness with a tin shed and a flag-pole lost in it," and then the landing of soldiers—"to take care of the custom-house clerks, presumably." We interpret Marlow's way of mocking the colonial attempt as nothing less than savage irony.

Marlow speaks in this way in order to unburden himself of his savage bitterness at the greedy, colonial invasion that brings death with it. He reveals himself as a moralist, a good man who recognizes and condemns the "sinister back-cloth" against which the "merry dance of death and trade is carried out." When Marlow says that ". . . idleness . . . seemed to keep [him] away from . . . truth," he touches on the important recurring work motif. To Marlow, as to Conrad, work is always equated with truth and reality. In his enforced idleness, Marlow loses touch with reality, regaining "momentary contact" with it only when he catches sight of a boat "paddled by black fellows," who are "a comfort to look at."

The Man-of-War: The incident which Marlow recounts of the man-of-war shelling the bush is almost a surrealistic image. Certainly, it is another indictment of the colonial capitalism Conrad saw as being heartless and hostile to the point of absurdity. It seems to Marlow that this "firing into a continent" is a touch of insanity.

The Swedish Captain's Story: The story of the hanged Swede is another instance of what emerges as a death motif, linked to the imagery of bone (ivory is dental bone), sepulchres whited on top but with dead bones inside and the death of Fresleven. This story provides an obvious link, too, with the doctor's advice to Marlow to keep calm. The suicide of the Swede illustrates the vengeance taken by the land on its invaders. Symbolically, the same toll may be taken when one confronts the very nature of one's being and questions what lies at its heart.

Nature herself had tried to ward off intruders.

Nature, here, is the coast of Africa, the edge of the jungle. The jungle is the "heart of darkness," the heart of man, or the hidden darkness in man, the lower or subconscious level of the mind. The subconscious does not yield its secrets easily; it defends itself against invasion. The mind is a very private place.

SCENE 4
The Outer Station

Summary

Here the scene becomes truly nightmarish as Marlow experiences his first encounter with the land itself, and its exploitation. A boiler wallows in the grass, an undersized railway-truck lies on its back with its wheels in the air. Pieces of machinery lie decaying and stacks of nails are rusting. Suddenly, with the tooting of a horn, blacks begin to run, and an explosion follows. No change is apparent anywhere as a result of "this objectless blasting," observes Marlow.

In clinking, single file six black men toil up the path. Each has an iron collar on his neck. Each is fastened to his neighbor by a chain. They are emaciated beyond description. They carry baskets of earth on their heads. Were these poor devils the

40

dangerous enemies, the criminals? Marlow asks himself. As the natives pass him in single file, panting, their nostrils quivering, and staring "stonily uphill," Marlow notes their "deathlike indifference." Behind them strolls "despondently" a uniformed native guard, holding a rifle which he hoists to his shoulder on seeing Marlow. Satisfied that Marlow is no enemy, he passes by with a large, white, rascally grin, seeming to accept Marlow as a "part of the great cause of these high and just proceedings."

Shocked and horrified, Marlow puts off climbing the hill until the native chain gang is out of sight. In by-passing an apparently purposeless hole in the ground, Marlow almost falls into a narrow ravine, where he discovers a mass of wantonly smashed drainage pipes. At last he reaches trees. He steps into their shade to be greeted by an "Inferno." The rushing noise of the rapids fills the "mournful stillness . . . where not a breath stirs, not a leaf moves." On the earth lie "black shapes . . . in all the attitudes of pain . . . and despair." Another explosion is heard. The "work" is going on, while these natives, hired "in all . . . legality," lie dying, diseased, starved, and lost.

Marlow hastens toward the station, near which he meets a white man, elegantly attired in the European fashion. This "miracle" is the chief accountant. Marlow respects this "hairdresser's dummy" because he "keeps up his appearance" in "the great demoralization" that is the jungle. His books, like his clothes, are in "apple-pie order." By contrast, everything else in the station is a muddle, a chaos.

Marlow remains in this station ten days, an "eternity." To escape its chaos, he occasionally visits the accountant's office. Perched on a high stool, the accountant attends to his books, exhibiting annoyance at having to put up with a sick agent temporarily quartered in the office. The sick man's groans distract "his attention."

It is from the accountant that Marlow hears for the first time about Kurtz, a "remarkable person" who is in charge of an important trading post and who exports as much ivory as all the other traders put together. At this point a native caravan is heard arriving at the station, provoking the accountant to express his hatred for the natives because they disturb his work. He asks Marlow to tell Kurtz that in his, the accountant's, office everything is "very satisfactory." He predicts that Kurtz will go far, "be a somebody." The last glimpse Marlow has of the station is a scene of ironic contrast. As the flies buzz over the dying agent, the accountant continues "making correct entries of perfectly correct transactions." And fifty feet below, Marlow glimpses the "tree tops of the grove of death."

Commentary

In Scene 4 we finally arrive in the heart of darkness, and encounter the full nightmare of waste, folly, inhumanity and death.

The "grove of death" is Marlow's first appreciation of the "sinister back-cloth" against which the "merry dance of death and trade" is played out. The "work" the Company professes to do is carried on here, but it is shown to be absurdly inefficient as well as a callous, heartless enterprise. Blasting goes on—but it is objectless." Machinery is there, rusting and useless, reminding Marlow of dead carcasses. Brutalized blacks stare stonily.

Conrad dramatizes his theme of an unnatural and absurd world where men have become as hard and metallic as machines and machines have taken on a devilish life of their own. The material image is one with the human image. In this surrealist yoking of the human with the inhuman, Conrad dramatizes the loss of heart and responsibility. As one critic puts it, *Heart of Darkness* closes out the nineteenth century with a resounding shriek of moral disapproval. On the level of parable, this scene offers evidence of Conrad's pessimistic attitude regarding the recurrent theme of man's inhumanity to man.

On the epic level, we begin to see in this scene a structural resemblance to Dante's *Inferno*. In fact, that resemblance is apparent even before Marlow's arrival at this first station during his epic descent into hell—the same journey undertaken in Dante's poem. For instance, the businessmen aboard the *Nellie* in the very first scene fit the structural scheme of Dante's poem, for they belong in Dante's Vestibule as men who, having abandoned the sea, now steer a safe middle course, their lives warranting neither great praise nor great blame. In the same way, the continentals Marlow meets are passive agents of the hellish exploitation to which they have lent their efforts. And so they, too, belong in or near Dante's Vestibule. Both the aunt and Kurtz's Intended are, in a sense, damned to inhabit a vestibule of their own making, an illusionary threshold to the real world. *Heart of Darkness*, in its "pre-Africa" stage, partially parallels the Vestibule stage of the *Inferno*. However, from the time Marlow lands in Africa the relationship to the *Inferno* becomes explicit. Africa's outer station is Dante's Limbo.

Note several important examples of foreshadowing. Marlow sees the chain gang and predicts that he will "become acquainted with a flabby . . . devil. . . ." This is the manager whom we meet later as the chief hollow man among the hollow pilgrims. And here for the first time, Marlow is told about Kurtz by the accountant. It is in the significant setting of the "grove of death" that this first disclosure of the "remarkable" Kurtz is made—and in the presence of the flies buzzing over a dying agent. From this first brief bit of information about Kurtz, Conrad will tease, sustain and feed our interest in him, creating an aura of mystery and suspense, which is climaxed by Marlow's meeting with him in Part III. As we shall see, we are never given a clear description of Kurtz, this vagueness adding to his shadowy quality.

SCENE 5

The Central Station

Summary

The next day, accompanied by sixty natives, each carrying a sixty-pound load, Marlow leaves the outer station for a two-hundred mile trek. Paths are everywhere but not a single native resident is to be met, though they pass abandoned villages en route. The routine of the daily march continues: "Camp, cook, sleep, strike camp, march." And always a "great silence" everywhere. Or, at times the sound of far-off drums, a "weird, appealing, suggestive, and wild" sound.

On one occasion, Marlow meets a white man in an un-buttoned uniform, very friendly, "not to say drunk," who informs Marlow that he is attending to road upkeep. There is no evidence of this, unless a "middle-aged negro" corpse, which Marlow stumbles on later, can be called an "improvement." A corpulent white man in Marlow's caravan habitually faints so that he has to be carried in a hammock by the resentful natives who drop him in the bush and disappear. At this juncture,

Marlow is reminded of the old Brussels doctor's wish to observe the "mental changes of individuals on the spot."

On the fifteenth day of the trek Marlow "hobbles" into the central station. One glance suffices to tell him a "flabby devil" is in charge. Carrying long staves, white men "languidly" appear to take a look at Marlow, disappearing thereafter. One of these, a stout chap with a black moustache, excitedly informs Marlow that his—Marlow's—steamer lies at the bottom of the river. Amazed, Marlow asks: "What, how, why?" "Oh, it is all right," the stout man informs him; the manager himself was there when the accident occurred and everyone behaved "splendidly." And now, the manager is waiting to see Marlow.

At the time, the "real significance" of the wrecked ship escaped Marlow. Now, as he narrates the story, Marlow fancies he understands what happened then. "Certainly the affair was too stupid . . . to be altogether natural." Marlow wonders what to do, now that the boat is lost. The very next day he sets to the task of retrieving the vessel and repairing it.

Marlow's initial interview with the manager is "curious," for the latter does not even extend the courtesy of asking Marlow to sit down after his twenty-mile walk. The manager, a common trader, inspires "neither love nor fear, nor even respect." What he does inspire is uneasiness. He has no ability for organization, no initiative, no sense of order, no learning, no intelligence. What he does possess—and perhaps this is the reason for his position—is "triumphant health . . . a kind of power in itself." He keeps things going. But he is "great" in that it is impossible to discern what controls him—that is the manager's well-kept secret. Marlow describes the manager as, perhaps, merely "empty" (in the sense that he lacks humanity and compassion), a suspicion that makes "one pause—for out there there were no external checks."

The manager begins to speak as soon as he sees Marlow, accusing him of having been "long on the road." The manager had been forced to start without Marlow. He had to push on to the upriver stations to "relieve" them. He was worried as to who was still alive. Nervously playing with a stick, the manager pays no attention to Marlow's explanations. The situation is "very grave, very grave." Rumor has it that Mr. Kurtz is ill. Irritated, Marlow interrupts the manager to inform him that he has heard of Kurtz on the coast. "Ah, so they talk of him down there," mutters the manager to himself. Then, curiously, the manager praises Kurtz to the skies, fidgeting and acting nervously all the while.

Savagely hungry—and angry—Marlow interrupts when the manager begins to question him about the length of time it will take to repair the boat. Not having even seen the wreck, Marlow is unable to say. The manager estimates that the job will require three months, at which Marlow flies out of the hut, calling him a "chattering idiot" under his breath. It is only later that it comes to him with "what extreme nicety" the manager had estimated the necessary time required for Marlow to repair the boat.

The next day, Marlow figuratively turns his back on the station by settling down to work on the boat, in distinct contrast to the pilgrims strolling aimlessly about with their "absurd staves." He detects the taint of corruption in the air which breathes the word "ivory." This, to Marlow, is "unreal," this "imbecile rapacity." The only reality is work. And "outside," the "great and invincible" wilderness, like "evil or truth" waits "patiently for the passing away of this fantastic invasion."

Months pass. Marlow tells us, "One evening a grass shed laden with calico, cotton print, beads and I don't know what else," catches fire. The stout, black-moustached trader comes "tearing down to the river" to get some water with which to douse the flames—holding a tin pail with a hole in the bottom. Everyone is behaving "splendidly, splendidly," he assures Marlow. As he approaches the fire, Marlow overhears the manager talking to an agent "with a forked little beard and a hooked nose"—reputedly the manager's spy. Marlow hears Kurtz's name mentioned and then something like "take advantage of this unfortunate accident."

The young agent invites Marlow to his room, which is furnished in comparative luxury, even to the extent of a prized whole candle. Supposedly, this bearded trader has the job of making bricks, but Marlow sees no bricks, though the trader has been here an entire year. It seems that all "sixteen or twenty" of the traders living here are waiting. All that comes to them is disease; all that occupies them is bitter backbiting and intrigue. Marlow senses the malignant "air of plotting" in the very air as unreal as everything else about the station and its traders—their pretence, "their talk, their government, their show of work." Their only interest is self-advantage.

As they chat, Marlow sees that the young agent is trying to pump him about his European connections, particularly those in Brussels. It is then that Marlow notices a small oil painting in the room, "representing a woman, draped and blindfolded, carrying a lighted torch." The background is "sombre," the woman "stately," the torchlight on her face "sinister." The painting "arrests" Marlow. He is informed that Kurtz painted it. "Tell me," he queries, his interest aroused, "who is this Mr. Kurtz?" "The chief of the inner station," he is told, "an emissary of . . . progress." And now Marlow is identified with Kurtz as "of the new gang—the gang of virtue," for, says the trader-spy, "the same people who sent him . . . recommended you." Marlow is suddenly enlightened; it is his aunt's "influential acquaintances" who have caused this rumor to spread.

Suddenly the young trader blows out the candle and they go outside, where the listless attempt to put the fire out proceeds. A native, suspected of having started the fire and beaten as a consequence, groans somewhere. The moustached trader appears, saying it serves the native right and that the beating will prevent further fires. In groups nearby the pilgrims, Marlow's ironic name for the traders, gesticulate with their eternal staves in their hands.

As the punished native groans, Marlow is importuned by the brickmaker not to give Kurtz a "false idea" about him. Marlow lets "this papier-mâché Mephistopheles" run on about his petty fears and ambitions. The brickmaker fears that a bad report to Kurtz might ruin his chances of becoming assistant manager of the present station. While this secretary-spy speaks, Marlow is keenly aware of the vast, brooding, primeval presence of the forest. What will be the outcome of the white man's intrusion into it? he asks himself. Who will emerge the conqueror, man or the forest? What is in there, he ponders. A little ivory—and Kurtz—Kurtz with whom he has already been identified but, whom he cannot as yet visualize. Nevertheless, he allows himself almost to lie to the prattling Mephistopheles by allowing him to believe whatever "he wishes to imagine" about Marlow's connections in Europe.

It is a strange omission on Marlow's part, for to him a lie has the "taint of death" about it. Somehow, Marlow believes his silence will "be of help to that Kurtz." Somehow, Marlow's identification with the as yet unknown Kurtz becomes much stronger, though the name Kurtz is just a word for him at the moment. At this point, Marlow speaks directly to his listeners. "I did not see the man in the name any more than you do. Do you see him? Do you see the story? Do you see anything?" It seems to Marlow that he is making a vain attempt to tell his listeners a dream, an incredible dream.

Commentary

Scene 5 is long and rich, rising to a kind of sonorous and symphonic pitch and intensity. It contrasts in its complexity of character and action with the simpler Scenes 2 and 3, which serve as thematic preludes to Scene 4.

A rough breakdown into subscenes is:
a) the trek to the central station,
b) talk with the manager,
c) repair of the wrecked ship,
d) the fire,
e) talk with the brickmaker.

Marlow's trek from the outer to the central station is through grass. Note the symbolic significance of outer and central. We are journeying inward to the jungle—the heart. We think back to the several grass images—grass through Fresleven's bones, for instance. Marlow meets other kinds of corpses in the grass—the lifeless ruins of abandoned houses. The grass image begins to gather greater weight. It is always connected with death and decay, and it is suggestive of life renewing itself even amid death and decay.

A word here about Conrad's style. An unusually constructed sentence like the following brings the reader up short: "Camp, cook, sleep, strike camp, march." This is pure imitative harmony—agreement of sound with sense—the monosyllabic verbs suggesting the very repetitions and plodding monotony of the trek itself. And a sentence or two further: "Perhaps on some quiet night the tremor of far-off drums, sinking, swelling, a tremor, vast, faint." Again we are arrested by the parallel poetic cadences of "drums, sinking, swelling, a tremor, vast, faint."

The incident of the white road-maintenance man is based on an entry in Conrad's diary of 1890: "Thursday, 3rd July. Met an officer of the States inspecting. A few minutes afterwards saw . . . the dead body of a Backongo. Shot? Horrid smell." One of the many recurrent death images, this detail illustrates the senseless cruelty inflicted by the white invaders. And again, Conrad has Marlow conceal his horror behind the mask of irony in calling the dead negro an "improvement" in road maintenance.

The inhabitants of the central station, manager and pilgrims resemble the fraudulent inhabitants of Dante's *Inferno*. The term pilgrims is an ironically accusing one, for these traders are travesties of the truly religious, their staves as falsely representative of them as they are. Their only religion is hate and cruelty; their God is greed.

The manager is jealous of Kurtz who poses a threat to his position. By the simple detail of the manager's discourtesy to Marlow when they first meet (Marlow is not invited to sit down after his twenty-mile walk) Conrad, in his usual oblique fashion, makes us suspect that it was the manager himself who wrecked the boat which was to take Marlow to Kurtz—and even fired the shed which probably contained supplies for Kurtz. The delay of the three months it will take Marlow to repair the boat will, the manager hopes, result in the sick Kurtz's death.

Marlow did not see "the real significance" of the wrecked steamer at the time, he says. (Another example of Conrad's oblique method of conveying information from which we gather that the manager had wrecked the steamer deliberately.) Next day Marlow goes to work on it, "turning . . . my back on that station." The "turning" of Marlow's back is another oblique reference to the important work motif that runs throughout the book—the motif of restraint which acts as Marlow's armor against the "imbecile rapacity" that "blows" through the central station—and through the hollow, corrupt traders, the faithless pilgrims. Contrasted with Marlow's conception of real work, the pail "with a hole in it" used by the pilgrims to put out the shed fire suggests, in an absurd fashion, the unreal futility of the work these white traders do. The "papier-maché Mephistopheles" is, next to the manager, a prime symbol of the kind of work done here. He is a brickmaker who makes no bricks. Instead the only occupation of these traders is "backbiting and intriguing"—again an unreal occupation to Marlow—and to Conrad—moralists both.

The several teasing references to Kurtz in this scene are brought to a sharper focus when Marlow notices the sketch in oils of the draped and blindfolded woman "carrying a lighted torch." The symbolism is obvious. The portrait represents Kurtz's initial idealism. He had intended to be a bringer of light to Africa. Instead, as we later learn, he has brought the darkest and most devilish of evils. But the brickmaker, unaware of Kurtz's corruption, describes him in terms of his original idealism as an "emissary . . . of science and progress." Conrad introduces the motif of identity, when the "Mephistopheles" identifies Marlow with Kurtz as being, like him, "one of the new gang—the gang of virtue."

Significantly, following this meaningful "lumping together" of Marlow with Kurtz, Conrad turns to a poetic description of the forest in the mysterious moonlight as spectral. The "silence of the land went home to one's very heart." The identification of the forest with the heart, coming right after the identification of Kurtz with Marlow, emphasizes the symbolic level of the story.

And now, with incredible subtlety, Conrad takes us just a step ahead in Marlow's journey toward Kurtz by having Marlow say that up to now Kurtz is just a name. He does not "see" him yet. The implication is clear: he *wants* to "see" him—to find him. This quest begins at this point to take on the quality of a dream. Again the subtlety is not lost on the reader. This is the archetypal journey into the self.

Note, too, the play of black-white imagery in this scene. The detribalized native is described as one of the "reclaimed." His grin is white and rascally, white here suggesting the dark "new forces at work"—that is, evil. Again, one of the dying natives in the "grove of death" has a "bit of white worsted" around his neck. Marlow wonders: is it a badge, an ornament, a charm? Conrad wishes us to connect that white with the evil in the "white" invasion that brings the native to this condition. On the other hand, black signifies the opposite of evil, for it is the "blacks" who suffer the "white" death. The accountant, too, is costumed in glistening white, reinforcing the symbolic meaning attached to whiteness.

SCENE 6
Rivets and Work

Summary

With the words "He was silent for awhile" the first narrator interrupts Marlow's account. On the deck of the *Nellie*, where the story began, it has become pitch dark, and Marlow is "no more . . . than a voice." It seems to the first narrator that the other listeners may be asleep for all the response they offer. In contrast, the first narrator tells us he is wide awake, hanging on to Marlow's every word and eager for any clue to the uneasy feeling the story has inspired in him thus far.

"Yes, I let him run on," continues Marlow about the brickmaker's prattle, "and let him think what he pleased about the power behind me." The brickmaker now attempts to put himself in Marlow's good graces, flattering himself and excusing and rationalizing his actions. Kurtz needs "intelligent men"—like himself—to work with; the implication, of course, is: won't Marlow put in a good word? No, continues the brickmaker, he has not been able to make bricks because of a "physical impossibility." And, naturally, he does "secretarial work" for the manager—a euphemism for spying—because no "sensible" man rejects the "confidence" of a superior. Doesn't Marlow see it, asks the "papier-mâché Mephistopheles?" What more does Marlow want?

Marlow wants to get on with the work of repairing his boat and he needs rivets, plenty of which are in the coastal station. He complains, suggesting some be sent up to the central station by carriers, adding that Kurtz would want just that done if he knew the situation. Marlow now suggests concretely that a letter requesting rivets be sent, but the agent says he writes only "from dictation." Marlow sticks to his demand for rivets, suggesting that a "smart fellow" could obtain them, but the agent changes his manner at this, and the subject as well, leaving Marlow abruptly after a brief while, but with a veiled threat hanging in the air. Unlike animals, no man bears a charmed life in this country, he states unequivocally in the moonlight, his hooked nose "a little askew" and his "mica eyes glittering." Obviously "disturbed and considerably puzzled," this "papier-mâché Mephistopheles" does not intend to help Marlow reach Kurtz.

With a sense of relief Marlow turns to his tin-pot steamboat on which he has spent many hours of hard and happy work. It is not that he likes work for its own sake, but for "what is in the work—the chance to find yourself" which is, to Marlow, finding "your own reality." Marlow now comes upon a chum, a white boilermaker, a "lank, bony yellow-faced man, with big intense eyes . . . an enthusiast and a connoisseur . . . about pigeons," a man despised by the pilgrims, but liked by Marlow who is friendly to the "few mechanics" in the area. Marlow shouts exuberantly at the boilermaker that they will have rivets, somehow. The two then dance a wild jig on deck, waking some of the sleeping agents. The clatter of the dance stops; the mysteriousness and silence of the vast land seems like a "rioting invasion of soundless life" ready to sweep all of them "out of existence."

Instead of Marlow's confidently expected rivets, the Eldorado Exploring Expedition arrives—"an infliction." It arrives in five separate parties over a three-week period, each led by a white man on a donkey, each consisting of "a quarrelsome band of sultry niggers." They carry a varied lot of camping equipment and other paraphernalia which look like "the spoils of thieving," so messy and disorderly is the appearance of each party. Marlow describes their talk as "reckless without hardihood, greedy without audacity, and cruel without courage." Their aim is "to tear treasure out of the . . . land"—like "burglars breaking into a safe." This "devoted band" is led by the manager's uncle, a cunning-looking, paunchy individual who resembles a "butcher in a poor neighbourhood," and who speaks only to his nephew.

Marlow stops worrying about rivets. "Now and then" he thinks of Kurtz. He is "curious" to see how an idealist like Kurtz, who has come to Africa "equipped with moral ideas of some sort," has managed.

Commentary

This scene is interesting from the structural point of view, for it demonstrates the first of several occasions when the frame breaks into the story of Marlow's trip. This means that the first narrator takes over from Marlow, so to speak. The effect of this is to give a sense of verisimilitude. Our imaginations leap back in time and space to the deck of the *Nellie* and, like the first narrator who addresses us directly, we realize it is dark and Marlow now only "a voice." Significantly, all except Marlow and the first narrator are either asleep or uninterested. In this oblique fashion, Conrad seems to indicate that the story of Marlow's spiritual adventure has no meaning for the three materialists, the director, lawyer and accountant.

After the short frame interruption, Marlow resumes his story. He is still hounded by the brickmaker who becomes very cold when Marlow demands rivets to repair the ship. Again, by having the brickmaker react in this way, Conrad tells us, obliquely, that the brickmaker is in league with the manager to prevent Marlow—and supplies—from reaching Kurtz too soon. The conflict between Marlow and the brickmaker symbolizes, too, the conflict between two sets of values: between the brickmaker's hollow inefficiency, and Marlow's ethic of work as an exercise in right living.

Tension has gripped Marlow since his arrival and the manager's unceremonious reception. He gives way to that tension by executing a jig with the boilermaker. In one sense, the dance suggests the possibility of Marlow's going mad in the jungle, as Fresleven did, and thus we are reminded of the doctor in Brussels who warned Marlow to keep calm. Marlow's jig—unusual for a man of such restraint—prefigures Kurtz whose corruption led to "unspeakable rites." But this jig is a civilized one, celebrating the possibility of getting rivets.

The Eldorado Exploring Expedition may actually be the Katanga Expedition of 1890. Conrad's true opinion of the rape of Africa by the whites is contained in his scathingly bitter denunciation of the members of the Eldorado Expedition. They are an invasion. They are a devoted band, an ironic term that links up with the pilgrims. They are "buccaneers . . . reckless without hardihood, greedy without audacity and cruel without courage." This incisive and poetic triad (three descriptive terms each consisting of an adjective modified by a phrase) seems to contain all of Conrad's ferocious loathing for the band of exploiters.

Marlow makes an important statement regarding work: it gives one "a chance to find [one]self." Here Marlow offers us an ethic, an ideal, for conduct. At the same time, it echoes the very theme of the whole book. Marlow is journeying to find himself.

The chapter ends with Marlow's increasing interest in Kurtz, who seems to be representative of the class of traders who have come to Africa with a sense of mission. Marlow is now very curious about such a man. How does his idealism fare in Africa, the symbol of reality? In other words, Kurtz will show how man's idealism stands the test of reality. The Eldorado represents the other class of traders, those who have failed that test and are there only for profiteering.

Part II: In the Heart of Darkness

SCENE 1
Prologue to the Trip Upriver

Summary

It is evening. Marlow is lying on the deck of his steamboat, when he hears voices. The general manager and his uncle, head of the Eldorado Expedition, are strolling on shore nearby. They stop close to Marlow, who unintentionally overhears their conversation about Kurtz. The manager expresses fear and hostility toward Kurtz who is exporting enormous quantities of ivory. He fears Kurtz may be promoted to his post. Both agree that Kurtz's popularity and influence is "frightful." The uncle poses the possibility that the climate "will do away with this problem."

Marlow, wide awake now, gathers from the bits of conversation that he overhears that about a year ago, Kurtz and a half-caste clerk had come downriver with a fleet of canoes bearing ivory, which he intended to deliver. After travelling three hundred miles, Kurtz had decided to go back, letting the clerk continue without him. This is an incomprehensible act to the manager and his uncle, who are "at a loss for an adequate motive" for it. As for Marlow, he seems "to see Kurtz for the first time . . . a distinct glimpse" of the "lone white man" in a dugout canoe, his back turned on headquarters and his face set toward the wilderness. Marlow himself is unsure of a possible motive for such an act. After all, Kurtz was out of supplies and so close to the central station. "Perhaps he . . . just . . . stuck to his work," speculates Marlow, "for its own sake."

The half-caste clerk has reported that Kurtz is very ill. As the manager and his uncle keep strolling back and forth,

Marlow overhears brief snatches of conversation—"Military post . . . doctor . . . delays . . . nine months . . . no news . . . strange rumours," suggesting that perhaps Kurtz's chances of survival are being measured against his not having been sent medical or other supplies all this time. The two now discuss a stranger, a man in Kurtz's district whom the manager wishes hanged "for unfair competition . . . as an example." The uncle heartily approves, saying that "anything can be done in this country," adding that the manager's chances for survival are excellent in view of his ability to withstand the climate, implying that Kurtz lacks this ability.

The two continue to discuss Kurtz, the manager protesting (too much!) that the delays which have prevented him from sending provisions to Kurtz are not his fault. The fat uncle offers a falsely commiserating sigh. "Very sad," he says. Now the manager touches on Kurtz's views that each station must be a "beacon . . . towards better things . . . a centre for trade of course, but also for humanizing. . . ." He chokes at the thought that a man of this idealistic calibre wants to replace him as manager! "Trust to this," replies the uncle, gesturing toward the jungle, and seeming to appeal to its "lurking death . . . to the profound darkness of its heart." At this, Marlow leaps up and betrays his presence. Pretending not to see him, the two walk away.

Commentary

There is structural parallelism between the openings of Parts I and II. Each begins with Marlow on the deck of a ship. This particular scene opens and closes with the mention of Kurtz. The very last scene closed on the note of Marlow's curiosity to meet Kurtz. Evidently, the subject of Kurtz is beginning to take on greater importance.

In characteristically oblique fashion, Conrad adopts the device of the overheard conversation to feed Marlow—and us—further information about Kurtz. The net result of the overheard talk between the manager and his uncle makes crystal-clear the conflict between Kurtz (contemptuously referred to as "that man") and the manager. We gather, as Marlow does, that the manager fears Kurtz to the point of violent hate. We learn definitely that the manager has intentionally delayed sending goods to Kurtz, hoping Kurtz will die. Most important of all, a real advance in Marlow's identification with Kurtz occurs when Marlow overhears the story of Kurtz's decision to go back to his inner station when almost within sight of the central station. Marlow attributes this to Kurtz's fidelity to work—an important Marlowian creed—and one of the book's important recurrent motifs. Thus, the illumination about Kurtz: Marlow says he "seemed to see Kurtz for the first time. It was a distinct glimpse." Conrad is subtly drawing Marlow, the outer man to Kurtz, symbol of his inner "heart of darkness."

The uncle's statement to his manager-nephew to "trust to this"—meaning the land—has a double edge, as almost everything in the book does. On the literal level, the statement advises the manager to hope that the land will be fatal to Kurtz. On the symbolic level, it suggests that the land is a testing ground, a symbol for reality itself. It is significant that Marlow uses the phrase "darkness of the heart" to describe the land in this scene. The phrase has reference to the river journey Marlow is symbolically making.

SCENE 2
Upriver Toward the Inner Station

Summary

The Eldorado Expedition goes into the jungle, there to be swallowed up without a trace, except that, later, news comes that all the donkeys are dead. As for the "lesser animals," as Marlow calls them—the men—no news is ever forthcoming. Nor does Marlow ever inquire. He is, at present, excited "over the prospect of meeting Kurtz." It will be two months before Marlow reaches Kurtz's station—the inner station.

They proceed upriver. It is "like travelling . . . to the . . . beginnings of the world." Silence, emptiness and an impenetrable forest greet them. They think themselves "bewitched and cut off forever" from everything familiar. Brooding, mysterious, and sinister is the impression Marlow gives of the landscape, the "stillness of an implacable force brooding over an inscrutable intention." But Marlow has no time to brood. His job is to pilot the boat, to "keep guessing at the channel . . . to watch for sunken stones." And so, attending to the "surface

55

reality," Marlow has no time for the "inner truth," which remains "hidden—luckily, luckily."

Nevertheless, Marlow feels the hidden forces lurking, their "mysterious stillness" watching him at his "monkey tricks," just as it watches his listeners aboard the *Nellie* on their respective tightropes for "—what is it? half-a-crown a tumble—"

At this dig the first narrator reports that one of the listeners growls at Marlow to be civil, indicating that at least one other, besides himself, is awake. And for that brief exchange we have been transported back to the deck of the *Nellie*.

Marlow resumes his story, apologizing to his listeners for his cynical remark about the price they receive for their "monkey tricks" by noting that the price includes heartache, adding that the price of the "trick," that is, our labors, matters little if the job is done well. This thought brings him to congratulate his listeners for their social efficiency, and himself, as well, for his efficiency as pilot, since he manages to steer his boat through various dangers, avoiding the "unpardonable sin" of scraping his ship's bottom.

Marlow has enlisted a crew of twenty cannibals, "fine fellows . . . in their place," who help aboard ship, pushing it when the boat has to "wade a bit." These cannibals, in Marlow's opinion, are "men one can work with," and men "who do not eat each other" before Marlow's face, as he puts it, having brought along a supply of evil-smelling hippo meat. On board, accompanying Marlow, are the manager and three or four pilgrims, staves and all.

The steamer crawls along upstream, for Marlow "towards Kurtz—exclusively." Occasionally, they pass a station out of which white men rush to greet them joyously, men who seem strangely "held captive there by a spell." The prime subject discussed during such meetings is ivory—and then the crawling is resumed "into the silence," into reaches and river canyons, past "trees, trees, millions of trees." And so the "begrimed" steamboat creeps, "like a sluggish beetle," making Marlow feel small and lost, but still with a residue "not altogether depressing," for they are making progress—slowly—toward Kurtz, penetrating "deeper into the heart of darkness."

Now, breaking the stillness, comes to their ears the occasional "roll of . . . drums behind the curtain of trees." What does the sound signify? War? Peace? Prayer? Those aboard do not know. They feel like "wanderers on a prehistoric earth . . . the first of men. . . ." And suddenly, rounding a bend, Marlow and the others glimpse and hear natives on shore—"a burst of yells, a whirl of black limbs, a mass of hands clapping . . . feet stamping . . . bodies swaying." What is the "prehistoric man" doing? Praying? Welcoming? They cannot tell, cut off as they are from understanding their surroundings.

The earth seems unearthly, yet the natives on shore are "not inhuman." Though they "howled . . . and leaped, and spun, and made horrid faces," it is their very humanity that is thrilling to Marlow. The "kinship with this wild and passionate uproar," between himself and the savages on shore, is a kinship which, he has to admit, is "ugly enough." But if one is honest, one admits a "response to . . . that terrible noise." "And why not?" asks Marlow. The mind of man "is capable of anything because everything is in it, *all the past as well as all the future.*" Here, in these natives, Marlow glimpses truth—but "truth stripped of its cloak of time." And one must be as manly as those on shore—must meet "that truth . . . with his own inborn strength." And, moreover, one must have more than "principles . . . acquisitions, clothes. . . ." One must have a deliberate belief.

At this juncture in Marlow's profound philosophizing a grunt of derision comes from his audience. "Who's that . . . ?" asks Marlow. "You wonder I didn't go ashore for a howl and a dance? . . . I had no time." Thus, Marlow explains how he quenched his savage instincts by immersing himself in necessary tasks. His job—surface truth—is enough to save any man, even a wiser one, says Marlow.

Another of Marlow's tasks is to look after the fireman, an "improved specimen," that is, a detribalized savage, a mixture of savagery and civilization, as evidenced by his filed teeth and ornamental scars in contrast to his job of attending to the steam and water gauges. Instead of living on shore clapping his hands and stamping his feet as a rooted member of a tribe, he is an uprooted mechanic, "enthralled to strange witchcraft," believing that an evil spirit lived inside the boiler.

When they are fifty miles from Kurtz's inner station they come upon a reed hut, a woodpile and a tattered flag on a "melancholy" flagpole. On the woodpile is a pencilled message on a board: "Wood for you. Hurry up. Approach cautiously." Something must be wrong further ahead, Marlow surmises, seeking clues in and around the hut. The table and book he finds testify that the occupant was a white man. The book, *An Inquiry into Some Points of Seamanship*, is at least sixty years old and looks like dreary reading. Marlow handles this "amazing antiquity" with great tenderness, for it has "an honest concern for the right way of going to work."

Absorbed, Marlow is only half-aware that the woodpile is being loaded aboard his boat. Suddenly he is startled. The manager and pilgrims are shouting at him, whereupon he slips the book into his pocket, feeling that to tear himself away from the book is like being torn from "an old . . . friendship." With ugly hatred in his glance, the manager remarks that the mysterious white man living here must be the miserable intruder he has heard about, adding darkly that even if the intruder is English, it will not save him from trouble.

The current is swift and the boat fights as if with her "last gasp." But somehow she crawls on. The manager displays a "beautiful resignation," while Marlow, by contrast, "fretted and fumed," wondering whether he is ever to reach Kurtz. But he experiences a sudden flash of insight: what did anything matter? The essentials of this affair lie below the surface of things, beyond Marlow's "reach . . . and . . . power of meddling."

Commentary

Four subtopics emerge as important dramatic focal points in this scene:

a) the symbolic descent into the self,
b) the work or restraint theme,
c) the detribalized fireman,
d) the manual.

The very first sentence of this scene bolsters the symbolic reading of *Heart of Darkness* as a descent into the primitive self: "Going up that river was like travelling back to the beginnings of the world. . . ." The mythic dream is explicitly suggested, as is the exploration of the subconscious levels of mind in: "There were moments when one's past came back to one . . . but it came in the shape of an unrestful and noisy dream. . . ." The potent and mysterious stillness which is that "of an implacable force brooding over an inscrutable intention" suggests, in those words, the mystery of the human heart which Marlow's outer journey into Africa symbolizes. As Marlow's own words strongly suggest: "The inner truth is hidden—luckily, luckily . . .. But . . . I felt its mysterious stillness watching me at my monkey tricks. . . ." This latter phrase "monkey tricks"— Marlow's ironic description of normal human affairs—brings on another frame interruption, when one of the listeners growls at Marlow to be civil. For that brief moment we are again transported back to the *Nellie*.

The symbolic subsurface of the story is revealed often in this scene, as, for instance, when Marlow says that for him the riverboat "crawled towards Kurtz—exclusively,"—that is, toward self-knowledge. This symbolic reading is reinforced when, a moment or two later, Conrad has Marlow saying: "We penetrated deeper and deeper into the heart of darkness." That "heart," we must by now be feeling, is the human heart, the primitive unconscious.

Most significantly, Marlow stresses the connection between himself—the civilized man—and those howling savages on shore, asserting that "what thrilled you was . . . the thought of your remote kinship with this wild . . . uproar." "And why not?" he asks, for "the mind of man is capable of anything." At this point Marlow enunciates the important principle of restraint that runs like a thread through his discourse. A man "must meet that truth (his own savage nature) with his own . . . inborn strength . . . a deliberate belief." And, in this statement, we see the recurring echo of Marlow's belief in the idea that redeems action, as he says in his musings on the Roman invasion of Britain in Part I, Scene 1.

"A fool," adds Marlow, "is always safe," meaning that the temptation toward savagery cannot tempt the man stupid enough not to realize it exists in him. Proof of Marlow's own inborn strength is his claim that he did not go ashore for "a howl and a dance" because he "had no time," a gruff way of saying that he bent himself to his work. This is another instance of this important work motif—the action part of the idea.

Marlow's ironic description of the fireman—"to look at him was as edifying as seeing a dog in a parody of breeches and a feather hat, walking on his hind legs"—tells us that here is another example of a detribalized native who breaches the ecological law that Marlow so respects. This fireman does not belong on board this steamer.

The manual that Marlow finds is another symbol of restraint and adherence to the task, that links with the work motif in this, and other, scenes.

SCENE 3

Before the "Attack"

Summary
Two days' travel brings them within eight miles of the inner station and Kurtz. Marlow wishes to push on, but the manager advises to wait the night out, not only because the navigation is dangerous, but because of the cautionary message. Marlow finds the manager's advice sensible enough, arguing with himself that it would take at least three hours steaming in the dark to cover the eight-mile distance and, besides, the ripples on the water are suspicious. Why is it, he asks himself, is he so impatient to proceed? After all, one more night makes little difference now.

Marlow anchors in midstream. Dusk comes quickly. The landscape seems immobile, the trees changed into stone. It is like a state of trance. The night sets suddenly, striking one blind. At sunrise, a white, warm, clammy fog rises, "more blinding than the night." At eight or so it lifts for a while, then sets in again. Marlow orders the anchor chain which he had begun to heave in, to be paid out again. Suddenly, a cry rends the air, a "very loud cry, as of infinite desolation," making Marlow's hair stand on end. The cry becomes shrieking, then gives way to silence. "What is the meaning—" stammers one of the pilgrims at Marlow's elbow. Two of the other pilgrims, scared out of their wits, rush out with their rifles.

The pilgrims are white-faced, fearful of attack and certain they will be butchered. By contrast, the "black fellows" are "essentially quiet," and, in reaction to the shrieking, exhibit alert, naturally interested "expressions." One or two even grin as they work. "Catch 'im," snaps one of the cannibals with a flash of sharp teeth . . . "Give 'im to us . . . Eat 'im." It occurs to Marlow that these cannibals must be very hungry. Their only food has been the rotten hippo meat which the pilgrims have by now thrown overboard because of the smell. The only other edible possessed by the cannibals is some "stuff like half-cooked dough, of a dirty lavender colour . . . wrapped in leaves."

Marlow wonders why these natives do not "go" for the whites "and have a good tuck-in." Their restraint is all the more amazing because they outnumber the whites six to one. Marlow, therefore, regards these "savages" with a new kind of interest, perceiving, at the same time, how "unwholesome" the pilgrims must seem to the cannibals, and hoping that he, Marlow, is not as "unappetizing." Added to all that, is the absurdity of the fact that the natives, though receiving weekly wages in the form of three pieces of brass wire, have been unable to purchase anything en route, either because there are no villages to stop at or because the manager has refused to stop when they did pass a village. In the light of all this provocation, Marlow cannot get over the remarkable restraint displayed by the cannibal workers, and wonders to what this should be attributed.

The manager now informs Marlow that he will be "desolated" should anything happen to Kurtz before they reach him. Oddly enough, Marlow observes that the manager is sincere, that he is just the kind of man who wishes to preserve appearances. That is the manager's restraint. The manager, therefore, wants Marlow to take the boat ahead—an impossibility, as they both know, because the dangerous channel is a "deadly place for a shipwreck," and because of the fog. After a brief argument between Marlow and the manager about whether to risk going ahead, the latter defers to Marlow, who, as captain, is in charge of navigation. But another matter concerns the manager. He asks Marlow if the natives on shore will attack, to which Marlow replies that the fog is as much a danger to the natives on shore as to the whites on board. But, more than that, Marlow senses that the cries of the natives on shore behind the fog, though "wild and violent," have in them an "irresistible impression of sorrow," a sense of a "great human passion let loose."

Now Marlow again leaps ahead in time to tell his listeners that, afterward, "what we alluded to as an attack was really an attempt at repulse," a purely protective action on the part of the natives on shore.

Commentary

In this scene, Conrad has woven together some important motifs:

    a) the obstacles in Marlow's way,
    b) the "cry",
    c) reactions of whites and blacks.

"Eight miles from Kurtz's Inner Station." So might read Marlow's log of the external journey up the Congo. Viewing the quest as a spiritual one of self-discovery, Marlow has almost reached the Kurtzian depths within himself. This deeper meaning is suggested by the very words Conrad puts into Marlow's mouth—a "dumb immobility" sits on the river banks. Every living plant seems turned to stone—it is the "stone age" of the self Marlow is approaching. The dusk comes "gliding in" long before sunset. They experience a condition "not sleep . . . [but] unnatural like a state of trance." Not a sound is heard. The sun drops like a stone beneath the horizon, striking them blind as well. The most significant detail of all, perhaps, to suggest the mythic legendary quest is the white fog which rises with the sun. The mystery they seek is very near, but very elusive, throwing up all sorts of bulwarks and obstacles before those who would seek to penetrate it.

The portents continue: a "loud cry, as of infinite desolation" rises from the natives on shore. On the realistic level, one interprets this as a wail of mourning that Kurtz, who has made himself lord and master over them, will have to leave, mortally ill as he is; or, perhaps it is a ritualistic cry before battle. On the symbolic level, however, this is the sad, mournful mystery of the invaded human heart.

The reactions of the whites to the possibility of native attack offer a contrast to that of the cannibals. The former are "greatly discomposed." On the other hand, the "black fellows" are "essentially quiet." What does Conrad suggest by this contrast? The cannibals, supposedly more savage than the civilized whites, show a curious restraint, "one of those human secrets that baffle probability." Hungry as they are, they do not eat their white employers. They have a code. Paradoxically, the pilgrims demonstrate a contrasting unwholesome flabby moral fibre that stamps them as less civilized in comparison with their

62

black slaves. These whites have no ethics, no code. Thus Conrad again evokes the natural law: the whites here are a completely "detribalized"—and demoralized—lot. The cannibals belong here and act out a social law of restraint and work.

The pilgrims fear an attack. But for Marlow, the "danger . . . was from our proximity to a great human passion let loose." The "passion" is in the heart's core. When let loose it may result in violence or in apathy. What Conrad suggests in this typically oblique statement is that when the evil in every heart's core vents itself without restraint, it produces one or two types of evil personality: the flabby manager of the pilgrim type, or the violent Kurtzian type.

SCENE 4
The "Attack"

Summary

The fog lifts. Two hours later, about a mile and a half below the inner station, the attack begins. As the boat rounds a bend, Marlow sees an islet in midstream, actually the head of a "chain of shallow patches" lying just underwater and resembling "a man's backbone . . . running down . . . his back under the skin." Since Kurtz's station is on that side, Marlow chooses to proceed up the western channel, which is deep enough near the shore to allow safe passage of the boat.

On the steamboat's deck are two teakwood houses, the boiler in the bow and machinery astern. Over all this is a light roof on stanchions, the funnel projecting through it. In front of the funnel is a small pilot house, furnished with couch, table, stools and a loaded Martini-Henry in one corner. This hut is where Marlow sleeps. Attending to the helm is a coastal tribe native, sporting "a pair of brass earrings" and wearing "a blue cloth wrapper." This native is, in Marlow's opinion, "the most unstable kind of fool" Marlow has ever seen, steering "with no end of a swagger" as long as anyone is observing him, but in an "abject funk" and completely unreliable when alone and unobserved.

Marlow is looking at the sounding-pole held by the cannibal and feels annoyed that more of it is showing every instant. Suddenly, the poleman lies down flat on deck, leaving his pole trailing in the water. The fireman sits down "abruptly before his furnace" and ducks his head. Marlow looks toward the river and is amazed to see the air thick with noiseless arrows. Quickly, he closes the land-side shutter of the little pilot house. The helmsman is now trying to steer while "lifting his knees high, stamping his feet, champing his mouth, like a reined-in horse." Suddenly, about ten feet away among the leaves, Marlow sees a native face looking steadily at him and, an instant later, makes out in the tangled gloom a swarm of bronze and glistening natives.

Marlow orders the helmsman, whose eyes roll in fear, to steer straight. The pilgrims open rifle fire, "squirting lead" into the forest. From the doorway, Marlow sees the arrows come "in swarms," looking, unless poisonous, "as though they wouldn't kill a cat." The natives on shore begin to howl. The cannibals respond with a war whoop. A sudden rifle report behind Marlow deafens him. The helmsman has fired the Martini-Henry, letting the boat twist. Marlow grabs the helm and crowds the boat into the deeper water near shore. Slowly, the boat drags along. The fusillade of arrows stops. Looking beyond the "mad" helmsman brandishing the empty rifle, Marlow sees shadowy forms running. Something big whizzes past Marlow. The rifle goes overboard and the helmsman, looking at Marlow in an "extraordinary, profound familiar manner" falls, rolls on his back and clutches at what seems to be a cane but what is, in reality, a spear stuck in his side. The helmsman's blood fills Marlow's shoes.

The arrows begin again. The helmsman stares at Marlow anxiously, gripping the spear in his side. Marlow jerks the steam whistle, which shrieks again and again. Then, as the yells from shore are checked, there arises from the forest a "tremendous and prolonged wail of mournful fear and utter despair." There follows a commotion on shore. The arrows stop. A few shots are heard, then utter silence.

A pilgrim appears on deck with a message from the manager but stops dumbfounded when he sees the helmsman in a pool of blood. Marlow and the pilgrim watch as the native dies without a sound or movement except at the last when he frowns heavily, lending to his "death-mask" a "sombre . . . menacing expression."

Marlow imagines now that Kurtz is dead, too. The thought gives rise in him to a feeling of "extreme disappointment" as if he has been "in pursuit of something . . . without substance." He flings one blood-filled shoe overboard, realizing suddenly that his sole purpose has been "a talk with Kurtz," discovering that, in his imagination, he has never envisaged Kurtz "as doing . . . but as discoursing." In short, to Marlow Kurtz has become a voice rather than a man of action, though Marlow knows that Kurtz has "collected, bartered, swindled or stolen more ivory than all the other agents together." What looms largest, however, in Marlow's imagination is Kurtz's "gift of expression . . . the illuminating . . . exalted . . . contemptible . . . stream of light, or the deceitful flow from the heart of . . . darkness." The other shoe follows the first "unto the devil-god of that river." Marlow, fearing that it is too late to hear Kurtz speak, finds in his own sorrow the same "startling extravagance of emotion" expressed by the howling savages on shore. He couldn't have felt worse, he says, had he been "robbed of belief" or missed his "destiny in life."

We are returned to the *Nellie* as Marlow responds with something like a burst of temper, exclaiming in reply to an interruption in the dark by one of his listeners: "Why do you sigh in this beastly way, somebody? . . . Absurd? Well, absurd. Good Lord! Mustn't a man ever—." Thereupon Marlow calls for tobacco. In the deep stillness that ensues, he strikes a match to light his pipe. His face, "worn, hollow . . . concentrated," appears, seeming to advance and recede out of the dark. He draws at his pipe, the match goes out and he reiterates his somewhat bitter condemnation of his listeners' failure to understand his feeling of desolation at the prospect of never hearing Kurtz, and how this feeling seems echoed in the natives' lament from shore. "Absurd!" cries Marlow again. "This is the worst of trying to tell. . . ." Here you are, he says, in effect, to his audience on the *Nellie*, safely anchored within society, with bodily sustenance and protection nearby, each of you with an excellent appetite and a normal temperature—in short, living a so-called normal, civilized life. Therefore, Marlow implies, their judgment can be of little value. After all—and here Marlow refers to the story proper—what can they expect from a man who has just thrown overboard a pair of new shoes? In fact, looking back, Marlow praises his own "fortitude" at the time, being then hurt and upset at the prospect of never hearing "the gifted Kurtz." But, as events prove, Marlow is wrong. Kurtz is waiting for him, though he has become "little more than a voice." Ironically, in the darkness aboard the *Nellie*, Marlow has become "little more than a voice," too. He becomes lost in thought, remaining silent for a long time.

Commentary

The death of the helmsman seems to dominate this scene, suggesting that Marlow is at the gates of Kurtz's underworld. In one sense, Marlow is the fabled prince trying to reach an enchanted princess in a fabulous castle. The awakening, however, will be Marlow's.

The fog lifts to reveal a sandbank chain that resembles a man's backbone. If any other equation has not proved that Marlow's trip up the Congo is a symbolic descent into the self, or a quest for understanding, this description of the land in terms of the human backbone should make Conrad's symbolism clear.

The death of the helmsman is important. First, he is another detribalized native, who, bereft of his roots, lacks the restraint of his cannibal colleagues. He lifts his knees, stamps his feet—and lets off the Martini-Henry at the natives—as do the equally and cruelly unrestrained pilgrims. In the midst of the helmsman's exhibition of unrestraint he is speared to death and Marlow's shoes fill with his blood. Note now how Conrad describes Marlow's action of throwing his blood-soaked shoes overboard. He "flung one shoe overboard" and became aware that what he had been looking forward to was a talk with Kurtz. The other shoe then goes "flying into the devil-god of that river." Marlow experiences a sense of disappointment. Kurtz must be dead, he thinks, and he will never hear him speak.

Conrad has piled mythic symbol on symbol. The fact that the helmsman's death immediately makes Marlow question whether Kurtz is alive shows a link between the helmsman and Kurtz and Marlow. What is that link? Think of the helmsman as the mythic guide to the underworld, which the hero (Marlow) will enter. Before this can be accomplished there is, usually, a token rejection of civilized man by the hero—Marlow throws away his blood-soaked shoes. Another interpretation is that, before the initiation of Marlow can take place, his guilt must be washed away by the ritual sacrifice of blood. In any case, it is fitting that blood should enter the drama just before the initiation ceremony. Marlow's thoughts of Kurtz at this point suggest all the more strongly that Conrad means us to interpret the helmsman's death and the flinging of the shoes overboard to placate some angry river god as a mythic ritual of some kind. Thus Marlow, Kurtz, and the helmsman-guide to Kurtz's underworld are linked.

Marlow expresses how disappointed he felt that he is not going to see Kurtz in these terms: "I couldn't have felt more of a lonely desolation had I been robbed of a belief or had missed my destiny in life." The reference to his "destiny" is clear: Marlow fears at the time that he will never succeed in delving into whatever lay inside him—will never confront the possibility of evil in himself of which Kurtz is the personification.

At this point, there is an important frame interruption. One of Marlow's listeners must have called Marlow's feeling absurd, proving that this one listener had never felt as Marlow did about the need to discover who and what he is. Marlow explodes at the materialistic listeners: "Absurd? Well absurd. Good Lord." And the next words we read are those of the first narrator, who describes the third of Marlow's lotus postures in the book. Significantly, there is a "flicker of tiny flame" as Marlow lights his pipe. Conrad habitually introduces points of light to light up his main characters who then sink back into the obscurity of darkness again.

SCENE 5

Approach to the Inner Station

Summary

Marlow—breaking the chronological sequence of his story and the silence at the same time—flashes ahead to events yet to come, exclaiming that he "laid the ghost of Kurtz's gifts . . . with a lie." This refers to Marlow's meeting with Kurtz's Intended, the fiancée whom Marlow meets only after his return to Europe. She, Marlow informs us, is "out of it," as are his aunt and all women, meaning that Kurtz's fiancée lives in an idealistic world of her own, and the men on board the *Nellie*, (so, by extension, all men) must "help them stay in that beautiful world . . . lest [the men's world] gets worse."

Roaming contemplatively over the past, Marlow comments on the very great contrast between the highly idealized view of

Kurtz that his Intended perceives and the Kurtz whom Marlow meets in the jungle, a "disinterred body." Kurtz had become "impressively bald," Marlow recalls, adding pointedly that "the hair goes on growing sometimes," suggesting by this that Kurtz is as good as dead, both physically and spiritually, when Marlow first meets him.

There are "heaps of ivory" in Kurtz's station. Kurtz intones that it is "my ivory . . . my Intended . . . my station." At the time Marlow meets him, Kurtz thinks himself lord of all he surveys. He has literally made himself "a kind of devil-god . . . taken a high seat among the devils of the land." But what, asks Marlow, despite all Kurtz's apparent power, possesses Kurtz at the time? This thought is enough to make one "creepy all over."

Marlow confronts his fellows on the *Nellie* again. How can they understand Kurtz? How can they, who live so securely and contentedly "with solid pavement" under their feet, imagine the "particular region of . . . first ages" a man may wander into by "way of solitude . . . and of silence, where no . . . neighbour can be heard?" These are the little things that make the difference. In the absence of a policeman and public opinion a man must rely on his own innate strength. A fool or a saint may never go wrong, the former being too foolish to know that he is being assaulted by the powers of darkness, the latter blind to anything but heavenly sights. But most of us are neither fools nor saints. And we must contend with realities, breathe dead hippo meat, so to speak, without becoming contaminated. There, Marlow philosophizes, is where our "strength comes in," the "devotion" to the "back-breaking business . . . of digging . . . holes to bury the stuff in."

Marlow affirms that all the foregoing is not to "excuse" or "explain," but to "account to himself for—for—Mr. Kurtz," who confides in Marlow, before he dies, something of his background.

It seems that Kurtz was educated partly in England and could speak English. His mother was half-English, his father half-French. "All Europe contributed" to his "making." Marlow now touches on a report Kurtz wrote, one requested by the "International Society for the Suppression of Savage Customs," a very "eloquent . . . too high-strung" document, seventeen pages long. But Marlow judges it must have been written before Kurtz's—"let us say—nerves, went wrong,"—

meaning before Kurtz yielded to corruption. It is a "beautiful piece of writing," filled with "burning noble words" about the possibility of the white man's bringing "practically unbounded" good to the natives, appealing "to every altruistic sentiment." Yet, at the end of the paper, like a "flash of lightning on a serene sky," is the postscript: "Exterminate all the brutes!"

Marlow considers Kurtz an unforgettable, uncommon figure with the "power to charm or frighten rudimentary souls into worshipping him as a deity." Marlow announces himself as Kurtz's "devoted friend," admitting that Kurtz has conquered "one soul in the world . . . neither rudimentary nor . . . self-seeking," meaning himself. No, Marlow cannot forget Kurtz, no matter what his worth.

And so, Marlow returns from his philosophical meanderings which are, at the same time, most illuminating to the story proper. He dwells for a moment on his regret at the death of the helmsman, who, though "a savage," and of "no more account than a grain of sand in a black Sahara," had "done something . . . had steered for me," while Marlow, in turn, looked after the native and worried about his "deficiencies." It had been a "kind of partnership." Marlow recalls once more the "intimate profundity" of the look "on the helmsman's face before he died," a look "like a claim of distant kinship affirmed in a supreme moment." Thus, Marlow affirms a sense of brotherhood with the savage, who, like Kurtz, lacked restraint.

Marlow now describes the simple, makeshift funeral of the helmsman. After jerking the spear from the helmsman's side, Marlow tips the heavy body overboard. It disappears forever as the pilgrims and manager offer a "scandalized murmur" at Marlow's action. From below, the woodcutters—the cannibals—offer their own "murmur" at Marlow's quick disposal of the body. To them, the dead helmsman may have been a "temptation." But, if the helmsman were to be eaten, Marlow decided it would be the fishes who would have him, not the cannibals.

Marlow takes the wheel, listening to the pilgrims, who have predicted that Kurtz must, by now, be dead and his station burnt. The red-haired pilgrim is "beside himself" with joy at the thought that the "glorious slaughter" of the natives on shore has, at least, avenged Kurtz. Marlow discounts this statement. The pilgrims are not only cowards, but shoot "with their eyes shut." Marlow is sure that it is the shriek of the steam whistle, not the rifle fire of the pilgrims, that caused the natives to retreat. Now the frightened manager suggests that they, too, retreat down the river before dark. Just then the buildings of Kurtz's station come into view. The manager, seemingly surprised, clasps his hands "in wonder."

Using binoculars Marlow sees a long decaying building on a hill, half-buried in the tall grass. Near the house are the remains of a fence, some "half-a-dozen slim posts . . . ornamented with round curved balls" on top. Surrounding all is the forest. But on the riverbank, Marlow sees a white man "under a hat like a cartwheel," waving to them. At the edge of the forest Marlow fancies he sees human forms "gliding." The manager screams at the white man on shore that they have been attacked, but the white man cheerfully beckons to them to come ashore.

The white man's appearance evokes a dim memory in Marlow of something funny he had once seen. The stranger resembles a harlequin. His clothes are covered with brightly colored patches. In the sunshine, he looks "extremely gay." He has a "beardless boyish face, very fair, no features to speak of . . . little blue eyes." He has "an open countenance." But the stranger's face darkens when Marlow asks whether they are on time, referring to Kurtz. "He is up there," is the reply, indicating the hilltop.

The manager and his pilgrims proceed to Kurtz's house, armed to the teeth, while the white stranger goes aboard the ship. At first, he and Marlow discuss the natives. Marlow is apprehensive about them. The white man says, in one breath, that it is all right, they are "simple people." In the next, he says that he himself has had difficulty keeping them off, but that they really mean no harm, that is, "not exactly." He "rattles away" at such a great rate, that Marlow wonders whether he "ever talks with Kurtz." "You don't talk with that man—you listen," is the reply, given with "severe exaltation," to be replaced, the next instant, by the "depths of despondency." Evidently, the stranger is a flighty fellow.

Gabbling confusedly, the harlequin reveals that he is a Russian sailor, the son of "an arch-priest," who ran away from home to gather experience, having set out for the jungle with "no more idea of what would happen to him than a baby." He has been wandering about "that river"—the Congo—for nearly two years.

When Marlow returns Towson's book to the Russian, he is overjoyed. The cipher, Marlow learns, are notes in Russian. Suddenly turning serious, the Russian returns to the topic of the natives, repeating that he has had trouble keeping them off. Marlow is curious about why the natives attacked his steamer. The reason, it seems, is that they do not want Kurtz to leave them. Suddenly, the Russian throws his arms wide. "This man has enlarged my mind!" he exclaims, referring to Kurtz.

Commentary

This scene consists mostly of Marlow's flashes ahead to his meeting with Kurtz's Intended. This is the elusive Conrad teasing us for page after page before he allows Marlow's climactic meeting with Kurtz to take place. The scene ends with a bridge to the next one—Marlow's meeting the Russian.

Kurtz has a "lofty fronted bone"—he is bald. Marlow says mysteriously that "the hair goes on growing sometimes." The reference to Kurtz's territory as symbolizing hell is clear. In hell lives the devil-god Kurtz—symbolically dead, a skeleton composed of nothing but dental bone. The greed for ivory has ruined him. Thus, the recurrent bone motif. And Marlow's reference to hair touches on the belief that a dead man's hair continues to grow after death.

Marlow's discourse on solitude is thematically important. Solitude "without a policeman" is man's testing ground where he must fall back in his own innate strength. Kurtz has failed this test; Marlow now faces it. The fool will not even recognize that the test is taking place—nor will the saint. But most of mankind faces the existential test of character in lives of action. For Marlow the forest will be the arena—the reality—where he will wrestle with the evil in himself.

Kurtz is given an international background. "All Europe contributed" to his "making." Conrad's intention is clear. Kurtz is a kind of Everyman and the Kurtzian possibility of evil is universal. Kurtz's report—its title is ironically significant—is a mirror of his progressive moral deterioration. Its intention is to help suppress savage customs and consists of an eloquent plea for a policy of good will toward the natives. Ironically, its author has turned to the deepest savagery in himself, to "unspeakable rites," and he has attached to the report a postscript which reveals his ultimate corruption: "Exterminate all the brutes!"

A large part of Scene 5 has been a "flash-ahead" to the Intended and Kurtz. Marlow resumes his story, returning to thoughts about the helmsman who lacked restraint—just like Kurtz. Action enters the scene again as Marlow describes the helmsman's burial. The inner station now comes into focus.

The scene ends with our meeting the harlequin, the type of fool mentioned, who—because he is a fool—is safe from Kurtz.

Part III: Out of the Heart of Darkness

SCENE 1

The Russian's Story

Summary
Marlow is astonished at the "insoluble problem" the Russian presents. It is inconceivable that the latter has survived thus far. His life hasn't been worth "a day's purchase," and yet here he is, "gallantly, thoughtlessly alive." Marlow admires and envies him his possession of the glamor of youth that urges him on and keeps him unscathed. Ruled by the "absolutely pure . . . uncalculating . . . spirit of adventure," a "modest and clear flame" that brings out Marlow's further envy, the Russian wants nothing from the wilderness but "space to breathe in . . . to move on . . . at the greatest . . . risk, and . . . privation." What Marlow does not envy is the Russian's devotion to Kurtz, a devotion "not meditated over," but rather "accepted . . . with . . . eager fatalism." This relationship with Kurtz, in Marlow's opinion, is the "most dangerous thing" in the Russian's life so far.

The Russian recalls, in a transport of joy, how he and Kurtz would spend days and nights in discourse, forgetting even to sleep, discussing everything, including love. At this, Marlow is amused. "Passionately," the Russian rises to Kurtz's defence. "He made me see things!" he cries, throwing up his arms. At this gesture, the chief of the cannibals fixes his "glittering" eyes on the Russian. The feeling overcomes Marlow that "never before did this land . . . this very arch of blazing sky, appear . . . so hopeless . . . so dark . . . so pitiless."

The Russian's on-going contact with Kurtz has been "broken by various causes." Kurtz would often be away for days, discovering "lots of villages." Because it was "dangerous to inquire too much," the Russian is vague as to the exact direction of Kurtz's explorations, whose purpose was to discover ivory. Though Kurtz had "no goods to trade with" as Marlow exclaims, the Russian's answer is revealing. Kurtz still had many bullets left. The implication is clear: Kurtz has raided the country, but not alone. The lake tribesmen worship Kurtz and, obviously, so does the Russian. Kurtz has come to the natives "with thunder and lightning," can be "very terrible" and cannot be judged "ordinary." For instance, Kurtz was once ready to shoot him, the Russian relates, for "a small lot of ivory . . . and there was nothing on earth" to prevent Kurtz from doing so. (A similar situation occurs later in the novel when Marlow confronts Kurtz in the jungle near the natives' fires.) Kurtz took the ivory and ordered the Russian to "clear out . . ." "I couldn't leave him," says the devoted harlequin, though, as he explains, he had to keep out of Kurtz's way until Kurtz became friendly again.

It was then that Kurtz became ill for the second time and, as in his first illness, the Russian nursed him. Despite this devoted care, however, the Russian had to keep "out of Kurtz's way," but he didn't mind because he felt Kurtz had "suffered too much." Though the Russian pleaded with Kurtz to abandon his way of life, Kurtz would disappear for weeks to "forget himself amongst these people [the natives]." When Marlow exclaims, "why, he's mad!" the Russian defends Kurtz "indignantly."

Sweeping the landscape with his binoculars during his conversation with the Russian, Marlow has the uneasy feeling that there are people lurking in the bush. The Russian explains that Kurtz, after an absence of several months—"getting himself adored," supposes Marlow, ironically—had come down to the river with all the lake tribe's fighting men, evidently to make another raid for ivory. Here, Marlow suggests sarcastically that Kurtz's "appetite" for ivory is now stronger than his "less material aspirations." But Kurtz has now become seriously ill and is lying helpless.

Marlow now trains his binoculars on Kurtz's house and sees no sign of life. He notes the ruined roof, the mud wall in the grass, the odd-sized windows. Suddenly, he brings a fence post into focus and is rudely shocked. He sees that the "round knobs" are skulls. These heads, Marlow judges, show that "Kurtz lacked restraint in the gratification of his various lusts, that there was something wanting in him—some small matter which . . . could not be found under his eloquence." Marlow further says that he thinks Kurtz eventually "found out what he lacked." But the jungle exacted a "terrible vengeance" for his having dared to invade it. It had whispered to him of "things of which he had no conception," and this had proved "irresistibly fascinating." The whisper had "echoed loudly" in him because Kurtz was "hollow at the core."

The Russian, crestfallen, assures Marlow that he hasn't dared to remove the skulls, for Kurtz's power is extraordinary. Even native chiefs crawl before Kurtz. At this revelation Marlow is suddenly and inexplicably furious, even more so than at the sight of the heads on the fence posts. He feels that the native savagery is a relief when contrasted with what he has just heard about Kurtz. The Russian is surprised by Marlow's reaction, forgetting that Kurtz is no idol of his, as Marlow sarcastically puts it, and forgetting, too, that Marlow has not been privileged to hear Kurtz discourse on "love, justice, conduct of life—or what not." The Russian protests that the heads belonged to executed rebels, at which Marlow laughs. "Rebels! . . . There had been enemies, criminals, workers—and these were rebels"—this is Marlow's bitter summary of the treatment of natives at the hands of the whites. The Russian tries to defend Kurtz again. Marlow doesn't understand how "such a life tries a man like Kurtz." His feelings becoming too much for him, Kurtz's last disciple, the Russian, confesses he is too simple a man to understand it all—that he is trying to keep Kurtz alive, that Kurtz has been shamefully abandoned.

Commentary

The entire scene serves as a prologue to the appearance of Kurtz.

From the point of view of dramatic necessity, this devoted harlequin serves as a source of knowledge about Kurtz, willingly revealing information about him to Marlow. Thus, curiosity is whetted about the real villain of the piece before he steps on stage. Another important reason for the Russian's appearing out of the jungle, only to disappear into it after speaking his piece, is that he is representative of that naïve segment of humanity who would follow a leader like Kurtz. In that sense, as the history of dictatorships shows, Conrad warns his readers dramatically that an eloquent voice, such as Kurtz's, can sway naïve and youthful people into the belief that he is rightfully "enlarging" their understanding.

Most of all, perhaps, the harlequin represents Conrad's youthful, adventurous, naïve self, juxtaposed against the older, wiser Conrad that the character of Marlow reflects. This opinion is substantiated by Conrad's constant stressing of the glamor that urged the Russian on, the glamor that kept him "unscathed," meaning unripe and unsophisticated.

That the Russian emerges spiritually unscathed after his long association with Kurtz—even though he claims Kurtz made him see things—is proof of the idea expressed by Marlow previously: only a fool and a saint are incapable of penetrating to the evil in themselves—that is, incapable of being corrupted by the eloquent Kurtzian voice.

The knobs on the fence posts turn out to be human skulls, "symbolic . . . food for thought . . . for vultures." It is interesting that Conrad uses the term "symbolic" in connection with Kurtz's evil handiwork. This substantiates Kurtz as a symbol for evil, itself. These heads are all-important in that they symbolize Kurtz's total lack of restraint. We see, clearly dramatized, the two conflicting forces in the book, the force of Kurtz, the temptation toward evil; and the inner strength, the restraint necessary to keep that tendency curbed. In Kurtz, there was "some small matter" (a typical Marlowian irony) lacking "when the pressing need [for restraint] arose." He had failed the test: the "wilderness had found him out," had rendered him as hollow as the ivory he had sought.

The scene ends with Marlow's sublime disgust at the death and havoc wreaked by the Russian's adored idol. The heads on the fence posts were supposedly those of rebels. Rebels, enemies, criminals, workers—these are the names assigned by the white exploiters to the African population they exploited. The political level of the story rises here with Marlow's raised voice. It is Conrad himself ending the scene with a "shriek of horror."

SCENE 2
Kurtz Viewed

Summary

The evening shadows have "slipped downhill" during the discussion. Suddenly a number of men appear from around the corner of the house, as though "from the ground." They "wade waist-deep" in the grass, carrying a stretcher. At this very moment a cry arises, piercing "the still air like a sharp arrow flying into the . . . heart of the land." In an instant the clearing is filled with "naked human beings" carrying spears. Their movement stops. All is still again.

At Marlow's elbow, the Russian offers a comment. If Kurtz "does not say the right thing" to the natives, he and Marlow are "done for." The stretcher-bearers stop, "as if petrified." The man on the stretcher—Kurtz—sits up. Marlow, resentful at being at the mercy of this "phantom," utters aloud the hope, cynically expressed, that Kurtz, who talks "so well of love," will spare them. Kurtz's thin arm rises in a gesture of command, his lower jaw moves in inaudible speech, his eyes shine "darkly," his bony head nods jerkily, grotesquely. Marlow pauses to reflect that Kurtz's name, meaning "short" in German is as true as everything else about him, for Kurtz looks about seven feet tall.

A deep voice reaches Marlow from the distance. It is Kurtz, shouting. The bearers take up the stretcher again and the natives silently vanish.

Some pilgrims behind the stretcher carry Kurtz's arsenal of arms. The bearers carry Kurtz aboard the steamer, lay him down in a little cabin and give him his correspondence. Marlow is struck by the fire of Kurtz's eyes and his "composed languor." Kurtz rustles one of his letters, looks at Marlow directly and announces he is glad. It seems someone has written Kurtz about Marlow, who is amazed at Kurtz's strong voice, "grave profound, vibrating," as if the man was "not . . . capable of a whisper."

Figures appear in the distance, two of them "under fantastic head-dresses of spotted skins. . . . " And then, on the "lighted shore," they see the movement of "a wild gorgeous apparition of a woman." She walks proudly . . . with a . . . flash of barbarous movements." She wears brass leggings and "innumerable necklaces of glass beads." She is "savage . . .

superb . . . magnificent," the image of the soul of the jungle, it seems to Marlow. She comes abreast of the steamer and stops to face the white men. Her face wears a tragic and fierce aspect of "wild sorrow and . . . pain mingled with . . . fear." She seems "like the wilderness itself . . . brooding over an inscrutable purpose." She pauses for a full minute, steps forward and stops again.

The Russian growls, the pilgrims murmur. With a sudden movement, the native woman throws her arms above her head "as though . . . to touch the sky." "A formidable silence" follows. Then, slowly, she walks along the bank and disappears into the thicket.

Nervously, the Russian announces that he would have shot her had she tried to board the ship and that he has been trying to keep her out of the house. Apparently, there is bad blood between the Russian and the native woman, but Kurtz is too ill to do anything about it. Just then, Marlow hears Kurtz's voice coming from behind the curtained doorway of the cabin where he lies, accusing the manager of wanting to save the ivory, not him. Kurtz promises to carry out his ideas, yet, in spite of his illness, in spite of the manager's interference. "I will return," he says.

The manager leaves the cabin. Kurtz is "very low," he announces to Marlow, heaving a hypocritical sigh, neglecting, however, to be "consistently sorrowful." The manager tries to put a good face on his efforts, saying, "We have done all we could for him"—an obvious attempt at rationalization. He accuses Kurtz of having done "more harm than good to the Company." They must move cautiously, continues the manager, because they must save the "remarkable quantity of ivory" in the district, which will be closed to them for a time. But their position is precarious because Kurtz's "method is unsound." Here the manager tries to pull Marlow into agreeing with him, adding that it is his duty to report Kurtz "in the proper quarter." For a moment, Marlow seems to agree with the manager, only to add that the brickmaker will "make a readable report" about Kurtz. Marlow's heavy irony confounds the manager, but only briefly. At this moment, Marlow feels almost nauseated; he has never "breathed an atmosphere so vile." He turns for mental comfort to Kurtz, saying, "Nevertheless, I think Mr. Kurtz is a remarkable man." The manager gives Marlow "a cold, heavy glare," replying "He was," and turns his back on him. Marlow's hour of favor is over. He is now considered, with Kurtz, as unsound. "Ah, but it was something to have at least a choice of nightmares," says Marlow, consoling himself.

As he says this, Marlow feels a sudden kinship, not so much with Kurtz, who is as good as buried, but with the wilderness. For a moment, Marlow feels buried, too, in a "grave full of unspeakable secrets." The Russian rouses him from his reverie by a shoulder tap and begins mumbling something about Kurtz's reputation. Marlow, urging him to speak out, says that he, Marlow, is "Mr. Kurtz's friend—in a way." The Russian suspects ill will toward himself on the part of the manager and his pilgrims. Marlow agrees, recalling the manager's earlier remark that the Russian ought to be hanged. "I had better get away," decides the Russian at this point. He has friends among the savages and there is a military post three hundred miles away. There is nothing more for him to do here, he says, but he is concerned about Kurtz's reputation. That will be safe, Marlow assures him, not knowing how truly he speaks. The Russian now reveals that the attack on the steamer had been ordered by Kurtz, who "hated . . . being taken away." But the Russian doesn't "understand these matters." It seems that Kurtz's intention was to scare the steamer away, hoping the whites would think him dead.

The Russian has a canoe waiting. He borrows cartridges and some tobacco from Marlow, sealing the transaction with a wink, as "between sailors." As he prepares to leave, he asks for a pair of shoes as well, and Marlow gives him an old pair. With one pocket bulging with bullets, the other with Towson's book, he seems to regard himself "excellently well equipped for a renewed encounter with the wilderness." The Russian's last words before he vanishes are about Kurtz: "I'll never meet such a man again. You should have heard him recite poetry," he says, his eyes rolling at the "recollection of these delights." That Kurtz "enlarged" his mind is his final word. Marlow wonders: did he really ever meet this Russian, this "phenomenon"?

Commentary

This scene serves to show Kurtz in his several aspects, rising to the dramatic climax of Marlow's further identification with Kurtz—the subconscious reality for which he has been questing.

The men carrying Kurtz in the litter proceed through grass, the ubiquitous living plant which, in the story, is always linked with death images. A cry accompanies Kurtz's appearance, piercing the air "like a sharp arrow flying straight to the heart of the land." This is a symbolic cry. The heart of the land has been pierced. Marlow has reached its depths: the corrupt, and corrupting, Kurtz.

That Kurtz is, symbolically, a resident of hell is suggested by Marlow's description of him as a "phantom," an "apparition"—terms suggesting mythic and epic levels of meaning. The "voracious" wide-opened mouth and the deep voice are prime aspects of Kurtz, symbolizing the voice from the depths of the human heart.

Another important initial impression: Marlow is struck by "the fire of his eyes and the composed languor of his expression." Critics have complained that Conrad contradicts himself in creating a Kurtz who, as the symbol of active evil, is yet as hollow as the manager, symbolic of passive evil. We see in the above phrase, however, that Kurtz possesses the entire range of evil: fire *and* languor. The suggestion is that Kurtz represents the possibility of any and every evil surfacing in the human condition.

The native woman represents the primordial depths, the "unspeakable rites" to which Kurtz has wedded himself. She is the image of the "passionate soul of the jungle." Just as Kurtz's Intended remains passionately engaged to the erstwhile, idealistic Kurtz, so this native woman is seen to be the reality for whom Kurtz has by-passed his Intended—who remains forever "intended" like Kurtz's idealism. The road to hell, Conrad illustrates, is paved with good intentions that are neglected or corrupted. Another echo of this motif of idealism tested and found wanting is Kurtz's report, which begins on an idealistic note but ends with "Exterminate all the brutes!"

In Marlow's discussion with the manager who "considers it necessary to sigh" when he tells Marlow that Kurtz is low, an important point emerges. So disgusted is Marlow with the manager's hypocritical sigh that, mentally, he turns to Kurtz for relief, praising Kurtz to counter the manager's duplicity by calling Kurtz "a remarkable man." When the manager turns his back on Marlow, the latter suddenly finds himself lumped with Kurtz. The identification of Marlow with his "secret sharer"— his inner self—is thus emphasized.

SCENE 3

Pursuit of Kurtz: The Confrontation

Summary

Marlow awakens before midnight and gets up to look around. A fire is burning on the hill, "illuminating . . . the station house," where an agent stands watch over the ivory. In the forest, wavering fires mark where the natives—Kurtz's "adorers"—keep their uneasy vigil. "The monotonous beating of a drum fills the air" with "a lingering vibration." A steady, hypnotic chanting emanates from the woods. Marlow dozes off but is rudely awakened by an "abrupt burst of yells" soon replaced by the "droning" of voices again. Marlow glances into the cabin. The light burns, but Kurtz is gone.

Marlow can hardly believe his eyes. He is "completely unnerved," extremely shocked and frightened. What made his emotion "overpowering" was the "moral shock," as if something monstrous had been thrust on him. This feeling lasts a "fraction of a second," to be replaced by a sense of danger, which, oddly enough, Marlow feels is a welcome substitute for his former panic. He does not raise an alarm—another strange reaction. Instead, he goes out to deal with Kurtz, alone, though an armed agent, who could help him, snores nearby. Thus, Marlow does not betray Kurtz; he remains loyal to the nightmare of his choice. Marlow never does understand why he was jealous "of sharing with anyone the . . . blackness" of his experience.

He sees Kurtz's broad trail on the bank. Kurtz is obviously crawling on all fours. Fists clenched, Marlow strides ahead. Strange thoughts come to him. He imagines the old knitting woman in Brussels—a "most improper person to be sitting at the other end of such an affair"—and her cat. Mentally, he sees again the pilgrims shouting at the natives. He imagines he will never get back to the steamer, that he will live in the woods until death overtakes him. And—strangest of all, perhaps—he confuses the jungle drumbeat with the beating of his heart.

Marlow is sure he will track Kurtz down. This he does by circumventing him, almost stumbling over him at the last. Unsteadily, Kurtz rises "like a vapour exhaled by the earth." Marlow has succeeded in cutting Kurtz off from the fires of the tribesmen. As he actually confronts Kurtz, Marlow comes to his senses, seeing the danger in his present situation. What if Kurtz shouts to the natives close by? In a whisper, Marlow asks Kurtz, "Do you know what you are doing?" Kurtz's answer—"Perfectly"—reverberating "like a trumpet" makes Marlow fearful. Should the nearby natives hear them they will be lost. Some "inspiration" causes Marlow to say the right thing to Kurtz. "You will be lost," Marlow warns, "Utterly lost." It is at this moment that the foundations of a bond between Marlow and Kurtz are laid—"to endure . . . even to the end—even beyond."

Marlow's warning seems to unsettle Kurtz, who mutters irresolutely about his immense plans and about having been "on the threshold of great things." The great things Kurtz has in mind make Marlow's "blood run cold." Desperately, Marlow threatens to kill Kurtz if he tries to shout. Kurtz mentions the manager, referring to him as a "scoundrel" but Marlow interrupts to promise that Kurtz's success in Europe "will be assured, in any case," attempting to mollify him for Marlow does not really want to kill him.

What Marlow is attempting is to fight the jungle for Kurtz's soul, "to break the spell . . . of the wilderness" that has awakened all of Kurtz's brutal instincts, has "beguiled his unlawful soul beyond the boundaries of permitted aspirations." Marlow knows full well how dangerous this struggle is, for he is dealing with a person to whom he cannot appeal "in the name of anything high or low." What Marlow has to invoke is Kurtz himself—his "exalted and incredible degradation"—that is, the evil lurking in Kurtz, the man who stands free from all judgment, the man who has "kicked himself loose of the earth."

The argument rages between Kurtz and Marlow. "If anybody ever struggled with a soul . . . !" exclaims Marlow, he is that man. Kurtz's intelligence is clear, but Marlow is convinced that his soul is mad, mad with having "looked into itself," while "alone in the wilderness." Marlow has a similar ordeal in looking deeply into Kurtz himself. In these struggles, Marlow with Kurtz and Kurtz with himself, Marlow sees "The inconceivable mystery of a soul that knew no restraint, no faith and no fear, yet struggling blindly with itself." Finally Kurtz is persuaded by Marlow to return to the steamer.

Next day, in full sight of the "mass of naked, breathing, quivering, bronze bodies," who have "flowed out of the woods again," Marlow steams downstream. The natives watch the steamer as if it is some fierce river-demon "beating the water with its . . . tail . . . breathing black smoke."

Three of the natives, apparently witch doctors, perform a wild dance as the steamer passes, stamping their feet, shaking feathers and gourds toward the "fierce river god" (the steamer) and shouting "strings of amazing words." The crowd of natives respond with "deep murmurs" resembling some "satanic litany."

Kurtz, from his prone position in the wheelhouse stares through the open shutter. The "woman with helmeted head," Kurtz's native mistress, rushes to the bank and shouts something that is taken up by all the natives. Marlow asks if Kurtz understands the shouting. A mingled look of longing, wistfulness and hate appears on Kurtz's face. He smiles a smile of "indefinable meaning." His lips twitch "convulsively." And he gasps out, "Do I not?" The words seem torn from him by a "supernatural power."

Marlow pulls the whistle string to prevent the pilgrims from shooting at the natives for a "jolly lark." The natives flinch at the sound. They run at the repeated whistle screech. But Kurtz's "barbarous and superb" native mistress remains, her bare arms "stretched tragically" after the departing whites. In spite of Marlow's attempt to stop it, the pilgrims begin "their little fun"—shooting—and the scene is blackened by gunsmoke.

Commentary

This scene, together with the next, is the climax of the book, for here Marlow pursues, confronts and wrestles with Kurtz. It is the symbolic inner struggle within Marlow himself that the action so dramatically—almost melodramatically—portrays.

Marlow awakens to the sound of drums—"like the beating of a heart"—the "heart of darkness" he has penetrated. When he finds Kurtz missing, he experiences a dreadful state of shock. He must compulsively seek out the missing Kurtz, the missing shadow within himself. "It was ordered . . . it was written I should be loyal to the nightmare of my choice," says Marlow.

Significantly, Marlow discovers in Kurtz's travel through the grass that Kurtz is crawling on all fours. The primitive self Marlow seeks is using the most primitive means of locomotion. As Marlow strides through the grass, he feels hostility rise toward Kurtz. The battle will soon be joined between the two.

He thinks of the knitting woman. This is natural enough for, as the mythic fate she personifies, she has knitted precisely this fate for Marlow; namely, that he will confront the Kurtzian self in the heart's jungle. Marlow's irony is never more in evidence, therefore, than when he calls this old knitting woman a "most improper person to be sitting at the other end of such an affair."

The symbolism becomes explicit: Marlow confuses the drumbeat with the beating of his own heart. Kurtz is heading for the refuge of native fires—his own hellfire. Marlow uses "inner strength"—ingenuity—to persuade Kurtz to stop. "You will be lost," advises Marlow—an irony, perhaps for Kurtz is already lost. In this way, however, an enduring intimacy is established between Marlow and the lost self, that Marlow, in his humane understanding of it as a "wandering tormented thing," rescues from further perdition.

The Kurtzian self now points wistfully to its immense plans, at which Marlow's moralistic hostility rises as an instinct to "throttle" that evil self "for good'—an ironic pun, perhaps. Marlow restrains the impulse, (illustrating that motif again) assuring Kurtz of his success in Europe. This pledge of loyalty foreshadows Marlow's defence of Kurtz's good name even to the point of the abhorred white lie to Kurtz's Intended.

Marlow tries to break the spell of the forest—struggles to redeem the Kurtzian self, perhaps, but Kurtz is beyond that. He has "kicked himself loose of the earth."

The struggle is now on the plane of words. Marlow struggles with this evil—but it is the dream-struggle, the struggle of the ego with the id; it has the "suggestiveness of words heard in dreams." Finally, Kurtz is seen as having had no restraint. Marlow knows that he, too, will have to go through the same struggle Kurtz went through if he is to emerge into full humanity. But Marlow will exhibit that little matter—the inner strength Kurtz lacked.

SCENE 4

The Death of Kurtz

Summary

The "brown current" bears the steamer downstream twice as fast as it struggled up the river. At the same time, Kurtz's life runs out just as swiftly, "ebbing . . . into the sea of inexorable time." Now the manager is content for the "affair" has ended satisfactorily for him. When Kurtz dies, Marlow will be the only survivor of the party of "unsound method," for he, Marlow, has been linked with Kurtz as one of the new breed of idealists. Marlow ponders: "It is strange how I accepted . . . this unforeseen partnership, this choice of nightmares forced upon me . . ."

All the while Kurtz cries: "A voice! A voice!" Kurtz's voice seems stronger than he himself, hiding in its folds the evil, the "barren darkness" within him. His talk is haunted by "shadowy images of wealth and fame." Now the present Kurtz—the "hollow sham whose fate it was to be buried presently"—finds at his bedside the "shade of the original Kurtz." The two warring Kurtzian selves fight for his soul, which is "satiated with primitive emotions, avid of lying fame . . . of all appearance of success and power." These warring twin selves are "diabolic love" and "unearthly hate" of the evil Kurtz has known, the mysteries he has penetrated.

As they steam back along the river Kurtz turns to childish fantasies. He wants kings to "meet him at railway stations after his return from fabulous trips to 'Nowhere'!" He is avid for recognition. But, of course, "you must take care of the motives—right motives—always," he says (an ironic statement for, starting with right motives, Kurtz turned to evil). All this time the steamer races along. Kurtz, looking at the landscape slipping by exclaims, "Oh, but I will wring your hearts yet!"

As Marlow looks down at him, Kurtz seems like a man "lying at the bottom of a precipice where the sun never shines." Nevertheless, Marlow has little time to spare for him. He is too busy "toiling wearily" to repair the steamer. Moreover, at times, Marlow is ill with the shakes and often "too weak to stand."

One evening, Kurtz remarks that he is "waiting for death." Marlow forces himself to reply, "Nonsense." But, he remains staring at Kurtz "transfixed." A change now comes over Kurtz's features such as Marlow has never before seen and hopes never to see again, and, fascinated, he gazes at Kurtz's expression, compounded of "sombre pride of ruthless power, of craven terror—of an intense and hopeless despair." It is a moment of "complete knowledge for Kurtz." And, as if looking "at some vision," Kurtz cries out, "The horror! The horror!"

84

Marlow blows out the candle and makes his way to the mess room. He sits down opposite the manager, who gives him a questioning glance which Marlow ignores. Confident and "serene" the manager smiles that peculiar smile of his, suggesting the "unexpressed depths of his meanness." Small flies buzz around the lamp and the men. Suddenly, the manager's boy puts his head in the doorway to announce with seething contempt: "Mistah Kurtz—he dead."

The pilgrims rush out to see. Marlow continues his dinner, but eats little. Ironically, he says that, because of this action, he "was considered . . . callous." Cryptically, Marlow explains his seemingly callous attitude: "There was a lamp in there . . . and outside it was . . . dark." From then on, Marlow ignores "the remarkable man who had pronounced a judgment upon the adventures of his soul . . . " Kurtz's voice— "What else was there?"—is gone. The next day the pilgrims bury Kurtz "in a muddy hole."

Commentary

Kurtz is still a voice, dreaming of the wealth and power he had sought to achieve. The two selves are there at his bedside, his original idealistic nature and the hollow sham he has become.

Some time later, as Marlow stares down at the dying Kurtz, he sees into the very heart's core of Kurtz. Revealed to him on Kurtz's "ivory" face is the very portrait of human depravity, "pride . . . power . . . terror . . . despair . . . desire . . . temptation. . . ." This is the secret Marlow has journeyed to find, dramatized here in Kurtz's last facial expression, the very definition of evil in the human heart. At this crucial point, Kurtz utters, "The horror! The horror!" Later, as Marlow dines (while small flies, that remind us of the flies in the accountant's room that were associated with death, buzz about) the announcement comes: "Mistah Kurtz—he dead." These two quotations are the most famous in the book.

Kurtz's cry has been much disputed by critics as another ambiguity. Perhaps Conrad is saying that, at the end of life the deepest self that has been committed to evil realizes the meaning of its acts and utters a judgment on them. Even if it is too late for redemption in this life, Marlow says later, the realization itself is a victory of some kind.

The manager best represents an evil of complete and flabby hollowness. Kurtz's is a result of his commitment to action. Marlow chooses Kurtz's "nightmare" as the less negative of the two.

SCENE 5

Marlow's Ordeal

Summary
 Now, just as Kurtz did, Marlow falls ill and wrestles with death. He does not "go to join Kurtz," but is "spared" to "show [his] loyalty to Kurtz once more." This struggle with illness causes Marlow to philosophize about life: all one can get out of it is self-knowledge that arrives too late to prevent the inevitable "crop of . . . regrets."
 Marlow describes his struggle with death as "unexciting" and taking place "in an impalpable greyness, with nothing . . . around . . . in a sickly atmosphere of tepid scepticism . . . without belief in your own rights . . . and . . . less in that of your adversary." Just short of dying, Marlow, unlike Kurtz, finds himself inarticulate with " nothing to say." By contrast, the "remarkable" Kurtz had something to say, "The horror!"—and said it. This was how Kurtz had summed up his life—had, with candor and conviction judged it, a judgment which had "the appalling face of a glimpsed truth."
 Here, Marlow makes a strange statement. It is not his own "extremity"—that is, his own struggle with death—he remembers best. Rather, it is Kurtz's extremity that Marlow seems "to have lived through," except that Kurtz "stepped over the edge"—(died), while Marlow has been "permitted to draw back. . . ." Marlow makes another of his deep pronouncements: perhaps it is in that moment "when we step over the threshold of the invisible" that "all wisdom . . . truth . . . sincerity" are compressed.
 Because Kurtz's cry at the last was "an affirmation, a moral victory," Marlow has been loyal to him, as Marlow's meeting with Kurtz's Intended in Brussels, the "sepulchral city," later proves.
 After a period of "time which I remember mistily," Marlow finds himself back in Brussels. He strongly resents the sight of ordinary citizens going about their ordinary affairs.

These people have not looked "over the edge" as Marlow has. Their knowledge of life, by contrast, is "an irritating pretence." When his aunt tries to "nurse up" his strength, he feels it is his "imagination" that needs care, not his physical self.

In the meantime, Marlow retains Kurtz's papers. One day a "clean-shaven man with an official manner" calls on Marlow. He is a Company representative. Gradually and insistently, he leads the conversation around to Kurtz's documents. At first, Marlow refuses to give them up. The official becomes "darkly menacing," arguing heatedly that the Company has every right to information about its territories. He further argues that it would be a loss to science "if etc., etc." At last Marlow offers him Kurtz's report on the "Suppression of Savage Customs"—without the postscript. The official reads it and, disappointed, hands it back contemptuously.

A second caller, Kurtz's cousin, a musician with "lank grey hair flowing over a greasy coat-collar" is anxious to hear "all the details" about Kurtz's "last moments." During the conversation, the cousin informs Marlow that Kurtz was "essentially a great musician" with the possibilities in him of "making an immense success," a potential which Marlow has previously in his narrative termed "extraordinary." Marlow interpolates another of his asides. He is unable to say what Kurtz's profession was—if any. That ambiguity is, perhaps, Kurtz's greatest talent, for Kurtz was a universal genius, capable of anything. When Marlow expresses this sentiment, the cousin blows his nose "noisily into a large cotton handkerchief" and leaves "in senile agitation" with some unimportant family letters and memoranda.

Third in the list of callers is a journalist, concerned about "the fate of his 'dear colleague.' " It is the journalist's opinion that Kurtz had been a born popular politician. This journalist, complete with "furry . . . eyebrows, bristly hair . . . and eyeglasses on a . . . ribbon," assures Marlow that Kurtz had been no worker but, rather, a born orator, with the power to sway audiences to any belief. Significantly, the journalist believes Kurtz could have been a "splendid" political leader of an "extreme party." The journalist is curious about what had induced Kurtz to "go out there." Marlow, in answer, hands the journalist Kurtz's "famous Report for publication." The journalist examines the document quickly and hurries off with his "plunder."

Commentary

There is much to illuminate the meaning of the book in Marlow's apparently offhand comment: "Droll thing life is—that mysterious arrangement of merciless logic for a futile purpose." We have here a definition of Conrad's pessimism. "The most you can hope from it is some knowledge of yourself—that comes too late—a crop of inextinguishable regrets." Marlow gives the clue to Kurtz's cry, "The horror! The horror!" Kurtz has achieved self-knowledge—but too late—and dies amid "unextinguishable regrets."

Why is Kurtz a remarkable man to Marlow? Why is Marlow loyal to him? What is the real nature of Kurtz's "victory"? These are crucial questions.

Marlow's "choice" of Kurtz is a compelling one from the very beginning of the story when he finds himself disgusted by the company for which he works. More and more, Marlow identifies with Kurtz, who, as an "apostle of light" is juxtaposed in Marlow's mind to the flabby pilgrims. The reason for Marlow's loyalty to his choice is that, evil as Kurtz is, he has discovered himself, become fully committed, even fully human perhaps. Through Kurtz's experience, Marlow learns what it means to act fully and positively. The only difference between Marlow and Kurtz is the little matter of restraint. That is why Marlow chooses another path of action. *But he chooses to act* as the hollow pilgrims do not. Only Kurtz and Marlow make the crucial breakthrough to self-knowledge. When self-knowledge is attained, so is freedom—freedom to do anything, good or evil, away from society's directives.

The above interpretation of Marlow's illumination borders on existentialist thinking. Most people—as Marlow's reaction to the people in Brussels shows—live in a dream world of illusion. So do the women in the book. Yet these illusions save most people from the blinding truth about themselves—the reality of what it means to be fully human.

SCENE 6

Epilogue: The Intended

Summary

Marlow is left with one remaining task: to hand over Kurtz's "slim packet" of letters and the portrait of the girl.

Marlow decides to give these objects up personally, perhaps out of curiosity to see the Intended, perhaps because everything else belonging to Kurtz has "passed through" Marlow's hands—"soul . . . body . . . station . . . plans . . . ivory . . . career." There remains only "Kurtz's memory and his Intended." These too, Marlow wishes to "surrender . . . to . . . oblivion," to forget.

As he stands before the "high and ponderous" door of a "house on a street, decorous as a well-kept alley in a cemetery"—the house of the Intended—Marlow experiences a sudden recollection of Kurtz, a "vision of him on the stretcher," his mouth wide open "voraciously, as if to devour all the earth . . . all its mankind." The vision seems alive, a "shadow insatiable . . . of frightful realities . . . darker than night." This vision seems to enter the house with Marlow, accompanied by all that once surrounded Kurtz—"the wild crowd of obedient worshippers . . . the forests . . . the beat of the drum . . . like the beating of a heart." It is like an invasion of "conquering darkness," a vengeful rush which Marlow senses he will have to combat, alone, for the salvation of his own soul. In short, Marlow feels the same identity with Kurtz that he felt in the forest, an identity that extends to feeling the same temptation Kurtz felt and to which he yielded. Marlow, however, will not yield. With a rush, all Marlow experienced when he met Kurtz comes back to him, especially Kurtz's last words, "The horror! The horror!"

It is evening as Marlow enters the Intended's house. The drawing room where he waits is "lofty . . . with three long windows . . . like three luminous . . . columns." The tall marble fireplace has a "cold monumental whiteness." The high door opens. Kurtz's Intended is all in black. She has been in mourning since Kurtz's death more than a year ago, would perhaps mourn forever, thinks Marlow, as she takes his hands in greeting. She is not girlish, but has a "mature capacity for . . . fidelity . . . suffering." Her glance is open and trustful. She seems to be "one of those creatures, not the playthings of time." Kurtz's death, for her, seems to have happened only yesterday, so deep is her grief.

During the conversation that follows Marlow's handing of the letters to her, the Intended is sure that it was impossible for Marlow not to admire, even love Kurtz. As diplomatically as he can, Marlow replies that Kurtz was remarkable. "You were his friend," she tells Marlow, her forehead "illumined by . . . belief and love." She feels she can speak to Marlow freely. The dusk deepens as she talks, "easing her pain in . . . [Marlow's] sympathy," talking "as thirsty men drink." She is sure that Kurtz "drew men towards him by what was best in them." She is fanatically sure that Kurtz possessed greatness. "But you have heard him. You know!" she cries to Marlow. With near despair Marlow ·is forced to "bow . . . before the faith . . . in her, before that great and serving illusion." The Intended bemoans Kurtz's loss to the world and to her personally. She is sure that something must remain. She cannot believe she will never see Kurtz again, "never, never, never." She stretches out her arms "as if after a retreating figure." As for Marlow, he is certain he will always see Kurtz's "eloquent phantom" as long as he lives and his Intended, "a tragic . . . shade," resembling Kurtz's tragic jungle mistress who also stretched bare arms toward Kurtz as he lay dying on the homeward-bound steamer.

Now she pleads with Marlow to relay Kurtz's last words. She wants something "to—to live with," for she "loved him." Marlow, pulls himself together and, speaking slowly, says, "The last word he pronounced was your name." The woman breathes a sigh, then utters an "exulting . . . terrible cry, a cry of unimaginable triumph . . . and pain . . . I knew it—I was sure!" she exclaims. Then she hides her face in her hands, weeping.

It seems to Marlow that the heavens are about to collapse upon his head, so guilty does his lie make him feel. He wonders what would have happened had he told her the truth— "rendered Kurtz justice." But he couldn't tell her that. It "would have been too dark—too dark altogether. . . ."

Marlow ends his story at this point. He sits apart, "indistinct . . . silent . . . a meditating Buddha." Everyone is still, the director suddenly breaks the silence. "We have lost the first of the ebb," he says. Marlow looks up. The "offing" is "barred by . . . black clouds . . . the tranquil waterway"—the Thames— seems "to lead into the heart of an immense darkness."

Commentary

The "inner truth is hidden" says Marlow, "luckily, luckily." Just as in the previous scene Marlow shows contempt for those blind citizens of Brussels who never achieve self-awareness, so he dramatizes his attitude toward Kurtz's Intended. Like the other women in the book, she lives amid lofty idealism, symbolized by images of heights in her surroundings. For her, the truth about Kurtz would be "too dark," thus, Marlow withholds it as being too frightening. This decision of Marlow's dramatizes Conrad's belief that, for most people, the reality of existence is too menacing, too dangerous. They live, instead, a lie, an illusion.

Character Sketches

Marlow

Marlow's Function

In searching for a device that would provide both form and shape for the novel, Conrad created his narrator, Marlow, and established him as the central character.

Marlow's function as narrator is dual. With Marlow, who plays the part in the book which Conrad played in the actual journey, Conrad had a mirror through which to examine the savage exploitation of the Congo natives and the degradation of Mr. Kurtz, the "hollow man." Indeed, from this point of view, the story is concerned with the effect of the Dark Continent on Kurtz and Kurtz's effect on Marlow. This is made clear by Marlow's own words:

> It was the farthest point of navigation and the culminating point of my experience. It seemed somehow to throw a kind of light on everything about me—and into my thoughts.

The equation between the "farthest point of navigation" and the "culminating point" of Marlow's experience typifies Conrad's method.

The voyage is at once a journey into the impenetrable darkness of Africa and into the darkness of Marlow's inner self. Marlow's function is not only to comment as a spokesman for Conrad's fundamental outlook, but to function as a character who is describing his journey of self-discovery, his personal growth of consciousness to the point that he ultimately becomes aware of authentic reality.

The particular point of view with which Marlow describes his journey to the Congo is one that views the past from the perspective of the present. In *Heart of Darkness*, it is what Marlow knows—the awareness that he has achieved through two separate experiences, one in youth (past) and the other in middle age (present)—that becomes the hub of the story. It is the older Marlow who acts as a refracting medium for these experiences. The reader meets a Marlow who, from his matured and objectified stance, is able to interpret and describe the younger man.

Finally, through Marlow, Conrad was able to convey the sense of human actuality, of the lived experience. Marlow frequently interrupts his narrative to take a drink, a smoke, or interpolate a remark. As a person who follows life wherever it leads rather than one who tries to change it, Marlow fits into Conrad's view that life develops upon a series of illogical experiences which are largely determined by chance or fate.

In contrast to the persons on board the *Nellie*, the seamen who have abandoned the sea and have become businessmen, Marlow is the only one who appears to have adhered to the true purpose of life—the development of ethical insight (awareness), and he is the only one who still "followed the seas," a distinction of symbolic importance. The other members of this group, unlike Marlow, are men whose lives have become complacent, almost apathetic. They maintain a vague tolerance that will neither affirm nor reject, approve nor condemn, a cautious cowardice in which no decision is ever final. At least one of them, the first narrator, is capable of sensing something special about Marlow. He relates that Marlow "had the pose of a Buddha preaching in European clothes and without a lotus-flower."

Marlow has embraced the inescapable darkness of life and has realized man's potential for both good and evil. As a consequence of this knowledge and experience, Marlow is able to exhibit his intuitive understanding of life and recount the journey into the "heart of darkness."

Marlow's Story—Public Level

On the more superficial level, Marlow's story is a record of things seen and done. *Heart of Darkness* is a sensitive and vivid travelogue which, while describing a journey, is an angry and satiric document on the absurd and brutal exploitation by European colonial powers, on "the vilest scramble for loot that ever disfigured the history of human conscience and geographical exploration."

Marlow judges the events from a position of detachment. Throughout the voyage Marlow is drawn both to moral idealism and to the values of order and justice. At the same time, he is repelled by their hypocritical abuse. Marlow comes on the scene "after a lot of Indian Ocean, Pacific, China Seas" and we feel that he represents, in his dealing with the Company, all the forces of straightforwardness and honesty. He can neither identify himself with the white men, because of their corrupt and destructive actions, nor can he identify with the black man, whose primitive existence is far removed from Marlow's European heritage. Yet, because Marlow abhors the white man's practices he turns from them for relief to the black man, who, at least, "wanted no excuse for being there." These men live according to a valid, uncorrupted code, a restraint which the white man, devoid of the social environment and order of his own civilization, lacks. Marlow, therefore, must strive to avoid, like the other whites in Africa have not, becoming detached from his personal, ethical standards, in order to keep a grip on his sanity and individuality.

His wonder and disgust at the "merry dance of death and trade" as he observes the anchored warship shelling the coast and her men dying of disease, grows even stronger on shore when he confronts the manacled negroes, worn out and left to die; the pointless blasting of cliffs; pointlessly abandoned shores; and stores that seem never to have been intended for any purpose. It is this inefficiency which revolts Marlow, as well as the cruelty toward, and exploitation of, the natives. He rebels against these conditions by refusing to become apathetic to them. At the central station he asserts his difference from the others by going to work.

Work is a form of restraint which, when actively exercised, is a principle of order and discipline. Because he maintains restraint Marlow is able to judge and condemn the white agents of the Company who do no work. He can recognize their petty schemes and their attempts to deceive; he can see through their mask of "perfect manner" and apprehend their laziness, their greed, their demoralizing and absurd behavior. He watches the flaming hut with common-sense detachment, knowing that there is no hope of saving it. As a result, he defines the ridiculousness of the man with the bucket who hopes to extinguish the flames. "I noticed there was a hole in the bottom of the bucket," Marlow says.

Marlow does not succumb to the nightmarish, farcical behavior of the Europeans. He retains standards by which he criticizes the traders, and the scope of his criticism is wide. It is from this same position that Marlow views Kurtz and makes his final choice of allegiance.

Marlow's Quest—Personal Level

On the fundamental and far more important level, *Heart of Darkness* is at once complex and ambiguous. Ostensibly, the story is of Marlow's quest for Kurtz. Actually, Marlow is questing for himself; he states often enough that he is recounting a spiritual voyage of self-discovery. "The most you can hope," he says, "is some knowledge of yourself." He remarks casually but crucially that he did not know himself before setting out. His journey, then, is one in which he gains both knowledge and experience, the climax occurring when he confronts Kurtz. When Marlow returns to Europe, he is a changed and more knowing man. Ordinary people are now intruders whose knowledge of life is to him superficial, and a pretence, because he feels "sure they could not possibly know the things [he] knew." The structure of this story, of Marlow's journey into the self or unconscious reality of existence, and the confrontation with this reality, is patterned upon the archetypal journey motif—the journey from innocence to experience, which is sometimes called the process of initiation.

The Process of Initiation

For our purposes, initiation can be understood to be the first real ordeal, crisis or encounter between the self and the world. Before this encounter, man is said to be in a state of dreaming innocence. He has not experienced suffering or guilt because he does not yet have the knowledge of evil and sin that exists in the reality of life. When a man does encounter this world he becomes an initiate who, through a sincere attempt to understand evil, passes from innocence into the state of experience. Being in authentic experience means being truly human. That is, man's emotional and intellectual capacities become fully realized. He knows himself; he is conscious of his identity in the world. The man who fails to become a true initiate will fail himself as a human being. He will not discover his own inner spiritual resources and will, eventually, degenerate into moral insignificance.

In *Heart of Darkness*, experience is identified with the most painful, explorative, responsible awareness. Marlow, made to confront evil, or the "heart of darkness," is also faced with the opportunity of gaining insight through the suffering and guilt that attend such an experience. He gains access to life, to the birth of consciousness, to the tragic knowledge of human limitation.

Marlow's principal symbol is the river voyage. The following describes the three crucial choices that Marlow makes in the story which, together, define his character. The first choice is made when he is in Europe; the second, in the Congo; the third and last, when he returns to Europe.

Marlow's First Choice

From the start, Marlow's quest had been the common egoistic quest for knowledge and adventure.

The first choice Marlow made in his quest was to go to the Congo because of his curiosity to discover what it was that "fascinated" him about this geographical region. The suggestion is obvious that he was tempted in the same way Adam was tempted by Satan, who resembled a snake, to eat the forbidden fruit. "The snake charmed me," Marlow says, as if the snake-like river was invested with some magnetically magic power. Indeed, since the traditional symbolic meaning of the snake is evil, Marlow reveals his innate quality of sensitive insight because he is able to recognize the archetypal embodiment of his fascination with the snake as a prelude to an inner, spiritual adventure.

The curiosity that characterizes his first choice also suggests Marlow's youthful innocence. In spite of his journeys to the "Indian Ocean, Pacific, China Seas," he confesses that he was "a silly little bird." He knows that he is naïvely ignorant of the nature of existence, conveyed by the image of darkness. As an innocent, he has still to discover the meaning of good and evil, to judge and redeem himself in a world of ambiguous and ominous portents. This is illustrated several times before he begins the journey. For example, when he encounters the two women knitting black wool in the Company's office in Brussels, he says, "an eerie feeling came over me." The women resemble the shadowy Fates who guard the gate between the world of civilized convention and the uncivilized world, between the conscious rational world and the uncertain realm which, in Christian terms, is equated with hell and death. As Marlow himself says, "I felt . . . instead of going to the centre of a continent, I were about to set off for the centre of the earth."

As Marlow proceeds on his journey, he becomes increasingly aware of his position in the world. He is alienated from the ordered principles of social environment and alone in his confrontation with the Dark Continent which he first observes from the boat. His alienation is further increased with the first recognition of the absurd and entirely irrational behavior of his fellow Europeans. The more he learns of their corruption, the more he is estranged from them, and the more he rejects the principles which govern their behavior. He tends to rely more and more on the values which he, personally, has acquired as a seaman, the values of duty, discipline and order (of which work is a symbol). These are the values learned through hardship at sea. While Marlow observes the conduct of the soldiers aboard ship, he senses a rapport between himself and the natural forces in the world, forces to which the soldiers, landing to enforce a so-called "civilized order" in the jungle, are alien. Marlow recognizes that there is an identification between the voice, the inner life of the jungle and "the truth of things." He is yet to learn that this same voice, as if tempting him as "a positive pleasure," contains also "The horror! The horror!" which finally becomes figured in Kurtz.

As Marlow gets closer to the mouth of the Congo he feels "a general sense of vague and oppressive wonder . . . It was like a weary pilgrimage amongst hints for nightmares."

On shore, the "hints for nightmares," and the growing sense of unreality, become much more evident in numerous portents: a discarded boiler and rusty rails, an upturned and useless railway truck, decaying machinery, the meaningless blasting of a cliff face, the terrible chain gang with that "complete, deathlike indifference of unhappy savages." Marlow is quick to perceive the degenerate condition of the white man and the savage and confused commercialism of colonization.

As he is gradually confronted by incidents that combine the horrible, the wicked and the farcical, in his progress toward the highest point of navigation on the Congo, he becomes aware of the necessity to affirm a conscious commitment to the inborn strength of his individuality amid the brutality of the Company representatives. He realizes he must not succumb to the nightmare. He must maintain a state of vigilance and judgment, not only over the perverted Company agents but, especially, over himself. Thus, Marlow emphasizes the necessity of restraint. This is not European social restraint which protects man from degeneracy with its laws and system of punishments.

This restraint is no longer valid in the wilderness of Africa. Rather, Marlow speaks of an individual restraint with which the work motif is associated. Marlow notes the various degrees of restraint and the kinds of work in the Congo. He admires the accountant, who, in the great demoralization of the land, attempts to keep up a semblance of work and order. He respects the cannibal crewmen who are actively engaged with work. Marlow, himself, forgoes diversions for work. Marlow is no longer innocent. He has embarked on a journey of knowledge and he must depend solely on his inborn strength to carry him through.

Marlow's Second Choice

While Marlow's initial choice was motivated by curiosity, his second and most crucial choice is made in the firm recognition that the "heart of darkness," represented by Kurtz, contains the forbidden, secret knowledge of reality, the truth that lurks behind the surface appearance of existence. It is a choice that Marlow must make. The extent to which he commits himself to the choice and its consequences, is the measure of Marlow's achievement of human awareness.

The "nightmare choice" which Marlow is compelled to make consists of Marlow's acceptance or rejection of the Company officials (the manager and the pilgrims), and Kurtz. Marlow, like Kurtz, is one of the new gang, "the gang of virtue" and, for Marlow, the unseen apostle of light, Kurtz, becomes the alternative to the apathetic agents. But Marlow is not trapped into an incredible allegiance. He knows what he is choosing, especially when he later makes his final choice. Nor is his an unconsidered attempt to escape from the moral decay of the hollow men; his choice is deliberate.

Even before meeting Kurtz, Marlow's choice is partly made. The manager and the pilgrims repulse him, and he finds himself, as a result, on Kurtz's side, opposed to the Company. But the question must be raised: Why must Marlow make "a choice of nightmares" at all? Why is he not able to reject both the pilgrims and Kurtz? The answer is simple. What Marlow sees as one of the nightmares is so compelling that he senses its investiture with truth and reality and cannot remain neutral or indifferent before it. Approving fidelity, order and discipline, of which light seems symbolic, he abhors dark disorder. But morality involves choice. Marlow's, however, is not between light and dark but rather between shades of dark. Compelled to choose between the pilgrims and Kurtz, Marlow chooses the latter because Kurtz, unlike the others, has embraced evil and is aware of the forces of good and evil in his own being. Marlow's choice is based on something positive, the good man gone wrong. He rejects the agents who, apathetically evil, are neither damned nor redeemed.

Moreover, not only has Kurtz discovered for himself the true nature of his existence but, also, of all existence. Kurtz has taken the fateful plunge into the universal world of the unconscious, the primeval world that determines conscious and rational existence. Marlow's illumination is a similar discovery about himself and all men.

Marlow's evaluation of Kurtz is ambiguous. He finds it hard to explain Kurtz and to justify the merits of his choice. He evaluates Kurtz through a series of contrasts and antitheses; contrasts between the evils of brutality, greed, hypocrisy and the evils that, at least, demand some individual action. Kurtz, compared to the "flabby, pretending weak-eyed devil" that the pilgrims represent, is a genuine devil, a god in his Satanic rites who acts through evil. The manager, ruled by pretentious caution, does evil by inaction. Kurtz can inspire a positive emotional reaction in Marlow, whereas the manager invokes only uneasiness. Kurtz commits himself completely to evil and, as a result, reveals to himself the "heart of darkness," the darkness of his own inner self. The manager keeps up appearances and can neither see the light nor the darkness. The evil of the manager and the pilgrims is not in their plotting, their opportunism, their neglect of Kurtz, but in their moral impotence. In Kurtz evil is incarnate, a passionate energy. With the others evil is a vacancy, an apathy devoid of existence. As a result, it is to the positive character of Kurtz that Marlow finally turns. What he learns inspires his illumination.

Marlow's Third Choice

Marlow has made his choice of nightmares. He has learned about his own capacity for evil and his capacity to resist it. He has realized that without involvement there is no restraint.

The consequences of this choice are two-fold. While Marlow has experienced an illumination and has discovered what it means to be human, this knowledge makes him a misfit in society. Back in Europe, he resents the smug faces of the people in the streets who are unaware of the challenge and the danger of reality.

Marlow is no longer naïve. He cannot identify with social codes and behavior because, to adjust to society, Marlow would have to reject his illumination. He would be false to himself. Unable to accept the illusions of the "sepulchral city," Marlow bears the burden of his knowledge, the burden of guilt and suffering that accompanies such knowledge, entirely alone.

However, Marlow's journey has not quite ended. In his alienated state, he must face one final test, a test which reveals Marlow's ability to maintain his illumination and also shows the compassion and humility that denote the true character of a successful initiate. The test occurs when he confronts Kurtz's Intended. Marlow's third choice, the result of the first two and, perhaps, the most important one in establishing Marlow's character, consists simply of either telling the truth about Kurtz to the woman or lying to her.

If Marlow tells her the truth he is, on the one hand, being honest yet, on the other, he is showing that he does not really understand the nature of his knowledge nor the responsibilities it entails. The Intended, a representative of the "sepulchral city," believes in an illusion. She loves Kurtz. Because she does not know what happened to him in the Congo, she loves a false Kurtz, a lie. However, if the truth is revealed to her she would not understand this knowledge of ugliness and evil. In fact, she might lose her faith, because the truth might make her unsure and doubtful of her beliefs. She would be in a state of uncertainty, unable to affirm her faith or reject reality. As a consequence, she would suffer.

Thus, Marlow deliberately lies. He does not want to disillusion her or cause her futile suffering. Marlow's choice confirms the knowledge he has discovered about himself, as well as his ability to exercise responsibility and compassion. He must live alone with the truth yet, ironically, the reward of his victory over the elements of evil is his knowledge of human limitations. Thus, while he repudiates Kurtz, he remains loyal to him. His loyalty acknowledges Kurtz's experience and hence the eternal existence of evil which must forever be encountered and conquered, always with the tragic awareness that defeat is possible.

Kurtz

The events and portents which occur before Marlow's confrontation with Kurtz are a preparation for the actual meeting between the two men. Through these events and the people involved in them, we, like Marlow, are introduced to the character of Kurtz.

The many references to Kurtz are vague and ambiguous. The first person who mentions Kurtz's name is the Company accountant, who describes him as "a very remarkable person." As Marlow proceeds up the Congo and draws closer to Kurtz's location at the inner station, "the highest point of navigation," we are made increasingly aware of the nature of this remarkability.

It is clear from the beginning that Kurtz's character, when he first came to the Congo, was not much different from the character of the new arrival, Marlow. The brickmaker identifies Marlow and Kurtz together as belonging to "the new gang—the gang of virtue." In other words, Kurtz, like the young Marlow, had been at one time an essentially good man. He was also an immensely gifted, vital, human being, "a prodigy . . . an emissary of pity, and science, and progress . . ." indicating that he had been invested with the virtues of his civilization, the technological advancements as well as the humanitarian attributes. Indeed, when Kurtz first arrived in the Congo he was an ideal European man, manifesting the best qualities of his cultural heritage—"All Europe had contributed to the making of Kurtz."

In part, it is these same qualities that have drawn the contempt and envy of the agents at the central station and have attracted Marlow's attention. Kurtz is sick. He has been neglected for a considerable time. Marlow is unaware of the extent of Kurtz's sickness and moral isolation but his curiosity about the man is intense. He anticipates some kind of instruction from Kurtz and, when he does finally meet him, it is evident that the event is the culminating point of Marlow's journey as well as of the study of the moral isolation of a man.

Marlow discovers that Kurtz has completely degenerated. He finds, on one level, a man who has committed unspeakable crimes against his fellows. On another and more important level, he sees a man who has totally succumbed to the irrational forces inherent in existence, a man who has allowed himself to sink to the darkest and lowest possible depths of evil. Furthermore, by observing Kurtz, Marlow discovers that in every man there is a potential hell.

Marlow realizes that Kurtz has been on trial in the Congo. His enlightened ideals and aspirations had been tested against the dark powers of the wilderness, and he had failed the test. He surrendered himself to these powers. Not only has Kurtz betrayed the humanity in himself, he has betrayed the natives and reduced them to poverty and subservience. Through him they have become tormented shades. He has deprived them of their dignity and will. However, he himself has been reduced to a shade, to a hollow man. Kurtz has chosen his destiny at the same time that he has been man enough to confront the evil within it. Unlike the agents who rejected the challenge of the dark wilderness, Kurtz has gone to the extreme in his exploration of the "heart of darkness." He has become, simultaneously, the victim and executioner of his actions.

Marlow, having the capacity to understand this evil and resist it, knows why Kurtz has failed. He knows that the result of Kurtz's trial reveals that this "remarkable man" lacks "some small matter which, when the pressing need arose, could not be found under his magnificent eloquence." This "small matter" is restraint. Kurtz, at the inner station is deprived of the supports and restraints of his society—"the warning voice of kindly neighbours whispering of public opinion"—the laws, customs, systems of reward and punishment prevalent in normal life. In this wilderness there is nothing to prevent him from killing for ivory. There is nothing to prevent his invading and plundering remote tribes, from exhibiting the decapitated heads of "rebels" on his fence, from being worshipped like a god by the natives in "unspeakable rites."

A fool or a saint, Marlow says in reference to Kurtz's white companion, the Russian, would be safe even if he were not protected by social sanctions. Kurtz, however, is vulnerable. He is driven by a monstrous megalomania. Ambitious for power and fame, he is blessed or cursed with an immense gift for eloquence. But his eloquence is worthless, a facade in relation to the wilderness and "the gratification of his various lusts." Like the helmsman, he has become "a tree swayed by the wind." Too late, he finally realizes he is deficient in inborn strength when he pronounces that "judgment on the adventures of his soul:" . . . The horror! The horror! Kurtz has discovered the truth about himself and thereby the truth about this wilderness. He has shown himself as a human being capable of both good and evil. His tragedy is moral because he has the capacity to act as a human being subject to no law or standard. His case is certainly instructive and prophetic. It has shown the inadequacy of the motives and aspirations of modern man without some kind of faith beyond a naïve faith in civilized progress and humanitarianism. But, it seems that this kind of instruction is available only to the few. Kurtz is the grail at the end of Marlow's quest and, of all those who come into contact with Kurtz, only Marlow experiences an illumination.

The Manager

The manager epitomizes the hollowness and moral impotence of the pilgrims, or the white Company agents in Africa. Marlow's appraisal of the manager serves as a sketch as well as a satirical comment on the European who has lost all human dignity and is perverted into a mere appearance of civilization. It is significant that the manager, like his cohorts, has no name, which further indicates that he has lost his individuality: "He was just the kind of man who would wish to preserve appearances. That was his restraint." It is this kind of restraint, a parody of a moral code, which excites Marlow's contempt.

The manager is rooted in a hypocritical, mean-spirited avarice. Unlike Kurtz, he is ruled by caution: "Cautiously, cautiously—that's my principle." He is never ill, never departs from his sinister routine of intrigue, never manifests a single sign of humanity. He has, in fact, nowhere to fall, unlike Kurtz who falls from a considerable height. The manager is apathetic. He does evil by neglecting the moral values and obligations of a human being. He is indicative of the "flabby, pretending, weak-eyed devil of a rapacious and pitiless folly," in contrast to the devils like Kurtz who, at least, demand some commitment to the self—a search into the meaning of one's own darkness. Hence, compared to Kurtz, who inspires a positive reaction, the manager commands neither hate nor love, but merely an uneasiness.

In terms of his position the inference is once again an ironic comment on the perversion and corruption of man and his relationship with work. A manager, he does not manage anything. At the central station, the location of his headquarters, a steamship has sunk in the river and, while cases of rivets were brought in to repair the ship, "there wasn't one rivet to be found where it was wanted." As manager, he is responsible for the inefficiency and general purposelessness evident in the corrupt morality and absurd behavior of his agents. This is in keeping with the reversal and perversion of values related to the manager's position which "had come to him . . . perhaps because he was never ill."

The Knitting Women

Marlow is disturbed when he is confronted with the two women who are knitting black wool "feverishly" in the outer office of the Company in Brussels. When one of the women glanced at him he sensed an "indifferent placidity" in her look, an "unconcerned wisdom" that "seemed uncanny and fateful." On the mythological level the women resemble Cirnaean Sibyle, who guards the gate of death and hell. This image is supported by the fact that they are working with black wool in the Company office, described as "a house in a city of the dead." The black wool gains an ominous meaning in that, while their work symbolizes sin and death, they are "guarding the door of darkness" of the Company offices, the Company that has built itself on the exploitation and destruction of the black man.

On the other hand, what purpose does the wool serve? We know it is not sent to the natives in the Congo, for Marlow's first contact with them is with men whose loins are bound in "black rags." Moreover, the white man has no use for wool in the Congo. Thus, the women's occupation becomes terrifyingly absurd.

The Doctor

The Company doctor who examines Marlow, is an ambiguous character. Once he has mechanically performed his official function he proceeds to pursue his private interest of measuring heads "in the interests of science."

His peculiar enterprise foreshadows many of the hideous activities pursued in the Congo. Compare Kurtz's collection of skulls and the implication of cannibalism associated with the natives, to the doctor's practice of carefully preserving the measurements of human heads, particularly those of men bound for the Congo. Despite the fact that the doctor's theory

104

involves the changes that take place inside the head, his interest in knowing these mental changes seems pointless since the white men who have gone to the Congo never return from there, or at least, he never sees them. The doctor seems to unconsciously, yet ironically, give Marlow advice by saying ". . . avoid irritations more than exposure to the sun . . ." and, "In the tropics one must before everything keep calm." The implication here is obvious. The doctor is advocating restraint.

The Pilgrims

The pilgrims are the human prototype of "the great demoralization of the land" of the Congo. As Company men they are identified with the "flabby pretending, weak-eyed devil of a rapacious and pitiless folly" that Marlow sees on his initial arrival in the Congo.

Isolated from the restraints and consolations of a social order, they are totally devoid of aims or values. They have degenerated into greedy, hypocritical and slothful phantoms who seem always to be "strolling aimlessly . . . in the sunshine of the yard" like hippos sunning themselves—except the pilgrims lack even such a dignity of purpose.

The image of death that accompanies the pilgrims recurs when Marlow wonders at the restraint that the cannibals exhibit. The pilgrims are hollow inside and hence they are unwholesome. They are a perfect contrast to the healthy, vital Africans.

The pilgrims, usually armed to the teeth, have become cowardly and cruelly destructive while retaining that most superficial and meaningless trait of civilization—perfect manners. Their hollowness is emphasized by the staves they carry. Staves, traditionally symbolic of authority and power, become, for the pilgrims, a crutch to support their empty mask-like appearance.

The Accountant

The depiction of the Company accountant, like many of Conrad's characters, is ironic. On the one hand, he symbolizes the outward manifestation of order and precision belonging to European imperialism. On the other hand, this appearance is recognized by Marlow as absurd, an illusionary facade in contrast to the dark jungles of the Congo.

The accountant is one of the first white men Marlow meets in the Congo and it is from him that Marlow first hears the name and the whereabouts of Kurtz. The efficient company clerk is first seen by Marlow as "a sort of vision," a "miracle." In the sweltering heat of Africa, stepping out of his office to get a breath of fresh air, he appears immaculately dressed in a high starched collar, white cuffs and snowy trousers. The white and brilliant perfection of his dress, symbolizing the thin veneer of civilization, is juxtaposed to the moral and physical degradation of the station, the inhuman misery of the black men who creep about in the shadow of the trees. The insensibility which confirms this fantastic external assurance of his culture is emphasized by the irony of his greatest achievement. He had instructed one of the native women, who "had a distaste for the work," how to starch and iron his pure white shirt-fronts.

The accountant's company function is just as absurd as his appearance. As the keeper of records, he has isolated himself from the surrounding demoralization by constantly keeping his books in "apple-pie order." This callousness is made evident by the fact that he was aware of the sufferings of the natives only when their noise disturbed his concentration on his books. He displayed no compassion for a dying man who was brought to the station and placed outside his window.

Yet, ironically, this man who looks like a stuffed "hair-dresser's dummy" perched on a high stool continually recording entries, elicits Marlow's admiration because, despite his absurd conduct, he has some order, some code, some commitment outside himself. This restraint Marlow recognized as essential:

> . . . in the great demoralization of the land he kept up appearances. That's backbone. His starched collars and get-up shirt-fronts were achievements of character.

It is this kind of restraint that the manager and Kurtz lack. It is better to live by an absurd code, like the accountant, than by none at all.

The Brickmaker

The brickmaker, like his fellow company agents, has no name, only a title. His title suggests that he is a builder, but he has nothing to build because the necessary material required for making bricks is not available. Indeed, "he had been there more than a year—waiting" for material. Yet, waiting for something was not an unusual practice for the white man in the Congo. To beguile the time the brickmaker outdoes his fellows in back-biting and intriguing to the extent that they are convinced that his real purpose in the Congo is not to make bricks at all but, rather, to spy upon them. In this hypocritical capacity, which he feels enhances his personal image with the Company, the brickmaker's schemes lead him to question Marlow and to be intensely suspicious of Kurtz. He seems to see this "new gang—the gang of virtue," as he describes Marlow and Kurtz, as a threat to his success. In fact, he "had been planning to be assistant manager." He fears that the coming of Kurtz has upset his plans as well as those of the manager with whom, it is suggested, he is in league. These suspicions indicate the acute insecurity and hollowness of the brickmaker's position. He fears that "the gang of virtue" might uncover his hypocritical and corrupt pursuits. Thus, Marlow, recognizing the brick-maker's machinations asks the question, which is no doubt true, "Do you read the company's confidential correspondence?" The agent turns the conversation to another topic.

The brickmaker not only has nothing to build, he does not even look the part. A brickmaker is a laborer; this brickmaker is an aristocrat. The contents of his hut are symbols of prestige and success, not of work. The "silver-mounted dressing case," a "half-pint champagne bottle," a "whole candle to himself" and the African trophies are indicative of his attempts to manifest an outward appearance of European order and culture. However, unlike the accountant, the brickmaker's appearance is entirely meaningless. At least the accountant maintains a semblance of work to justify his appearance, the other does nothing.

His facial features, the "forked little beard and a hooked nose" and "mica eyes," give him the physical attributes of a devilish figure. As Marlow himself says, he is a "papier mâché Mephistopheles," a devil of emptiness. Marlow feels that "if I tried I could poke my forefinger through him, and would find nothing inside but a little loose dirt, maybe." His behavior, like his title, is vague and thus menacing. There is nothing tangible about the man as there is with Kurtz.

Natives

The natives, unlike the whites, are not detribalized. They belong within the wild, mysterious surroundings of Africa. Marlow is quick to recognize this when he observes a boat being paddled by black men: ". . . they had bone, muscle, a wild vitality, an intense energy of movement, that was as natural and true as the surf along their coast." It is only when they come under the subjugation of the whites that they lose their vitality and become "grotesque masks"—the walking shadows at the station, brutally exploited and maltreated. They are symbolic of the pointless work of the white man in the Congo. There is a clear parallel between these "moribund shapes" and the "decaying machinery" (another instance of white man's loss of values) that Marlow finds everywhere.

The natives also fit into the general symbolic pattern of the tale. While the white man exploits and suppresses the black, the latter retains a nobility and majesty of humanity, finally reaping justice by absorbing the white intruder into the "heart of darkness."

Another example of the black man's superiority, even when it is a question of cannibalism, is evident in the episode where Marlow wonders at the restraint that the cannibals, who have been starving for countless months, exhibit in the face of temptation. These natives have some sort of moral code, a quality of restraint. Thus they define even further the white man's deadness, apathy and menace.

The Russian

The Russian companion of Kurtz is, like the accountant, an ambiguous figure. Marlow sees him as the prototype of youthful innocence who also, perhaps, has the capacity to recognize the "darkness." While the Russian's seeming naïveté might prevent him from understanding the diabolic nature of Kurtz, he suggests that Kurtz has "enlarged [his] mind," implying that he, acting the fool, is perhaps a wise fool.

His harlequinlike appearance and his unquestioned devotion to Kurtz, which he "accepted with a sort of eager fatalism," symbolize to some extent a wishful but superficial involvement which essentially covers up "his destitution, his loneliness, the essential desolation of his futile wanderings." Perhaps his outward appearance, while it intensifies the idea that he is isolated morally and vocationally (he was originally a sailor), save him from plunging into the darkness of moral chaos. In other words, by virtue of his clownish dress he is detached from the demoralizing environment.

Moreover, he, like the accountant, provides a certain link with civilization, a surface truth, or an outward impression of sanity in the midst of the impenetrable darkness. Like the accountant, the Russian maintains an illusion of purpose. This is revealed by the fact that he is the onwer of Towson's *An Inquiry into Some Points of Seamanship*, which, as a book on navigation, is a celebration of order, of sanity, "a singleness of intention, and honest concern for the right way of going to work. . . ."

Furthermore, while the manual provides a criterion by which we can measure the extent to which Kurtz has degenerated, it also provides the suggestion of a connection between Marlow and the Russian. The latter resembles the younger Marlow as an apprentice mariner who might have owned the Towson manual, the primary guide of seamanship. This view of the Russian as a projection of Marlow's youth serves to explain his very ironic existence: the disciple who responds to Kurtz's abundant proofs of cruelty and mean obsession with the steadfast conviction that Kurtz is a great man. Marlow, older and mature, can maintain that inner strength, that saving definitive belief that prevents him from having naïve illusions, which the Russian, because of his youth and innocence, cannot avoid.

The Intended

It is interesting to note that the female characters in *Heart of Darkness* seem to stand in a category of their own. "It is queer how out of touch with truth women are. They live in a world of their own . . ." says Marlow about his aunt. Considering *Heart of Darkness* as a journey of self-discovery, Marlow's assertion seems to deny women the right or the need for the quest for truth. Conrad has suggested an ironic ambiguity, a confusion of light and dark about their nature, although the women themselves are not aware of it. Marlow is only half conscious of this duality as his first reference to the Intended implies:

Oh she is out of it completely. They—the women I
mean—are out of it—should be out of it. We must
help them to stay in that beautiful world of their own,
lest ours gets worse.

Thus, Marlow tells a lie to keep the Intended in the dark by
preserving her light: "I could not tell her. It would have been
too dark—too dark altogether."

The ambiguity evoked when Marlow's lie is referred to as a
"saving illusion" becomes more explicit if we consider the
significance of the Intended to Marlow, who has recently
returned from the Congo.

The Intended is a spiritual person who cherishes an angelic
illusion of the beauty of Kurtz's character. This illusion brings
back to Marlow even more vividly the final invocation of
Kurtz—"The horror! The horror!" emphasizing the meaninglessness and futility of the truth to a woman who has no real self
and who has sacrificed all that is living in order to believe in a
dead ideal. She is so "thunderingly exalted a creature as to be
altogether deaf and blind to anything but heavenly sights and
sounds." Hence, Marlow's lie becomes a saving illusion which,
in turn, is ironically redemptive.

The Intended is a shadowy figure dressed in black. The
imagery associated with her reflects and alludes to the world of
the dead and, momentarily, Marlow sees her not as a creature of
light, but as a wild woman of the Congo. She imitates,
unknowingly, the gesture of despair the native woman performs
when Marlow last sees her on the river bank. In contrast to the
negress, the Intended is more pathetic than tragic. She is a shade
and in some respects as hollow as the white agents in the Congo.
Unlike the negress, she has disclaimed any kinship with ugliness
or evil; she indicates an unwillingness to face life. In spite of
Marlow's dull anger at her self-assurance, she manoeuvres him
to tell her what she wants to hear:

The last word he pronounced was—your name.

Native Woman
In contrast to the Intended for whom the "earth . . . is only
a standing place," the native woman signifies Kurtz's
passionate involvement with time and flesh. She is equated with

the vegetation of the jungle which stands for truth, for an amazing reality, which Conrad equates only with the African natives who alone are full of vitality. The ivory-bedecked African woman is the incarnation of primordial Time. She is the partner in Kurtz's plunge into the satanic "unspeakable rites." She is his native mistress, "savage and superb, wild-eyed and magnificent"—a prototype of the primeval, pulsating life-principle which, at the same time, is a lurking death. She is the goddess of fecundity who is idolized and worshipped, and the terrible queen who tempts man to his destruction and death.

The Aunt

Like the Intended, the aunt is separate from the darkness implicit in man's world. She lives in a special realm of her own and simply does not understand the real world. This much is clear from Marlow's comments about her. It is her world of illusions that provokes ironic reflections from her nephew on the feminine powers of self-deception. She is ironically described as the benevolent, self-righteous, civilized white woman living in the midst of trivialities: ". . . the excellent woman, living right in the rush of all that humbug, got carried off her feet." She talked about "weaning those ignorant Millions from their horrid ways." She believes Marlow is just such an "emissary of light" and with this belief she impresses his prospective employers.

Also reminiscent of the Intended is the aunt's characteristic of self-effacement. She seems to exist merely to be of use to men, rather than being an individual in her own right. With respect to promoting Marlow she says, "I am ready to do anything, anything for you." Moreover, because of her nature, she exhibits a somewhat misguided motherly protectiveness as Marlow indicates, "I got embraced, told to wear flannel, be sure to write often, and so on—."

She typifies the attitude common in Conrad's day of thinking of imperialist exploitation as something of a noble cause. Thus, she exists in the world of her illusions which are made clear to us through Marlow's irony.

The Helmsman

The helmsman exemplifies the power and domination that the Europeans exert over some of the natives in Africa, as a result of which these natives have become detribalized. The helmsman, "belonging to some coast tribe," is separated from the confines of his community. He works for the Company and is paid for his services, as is indicated by the pair of brass earrings he wears. He also wears "a blue cloth wrapper from the waist to the ankles," unnatural to a tribesman and suggesting foreign influences. As a consequence, the helmsman has deprived himself of his sense of dignity and harmony with his surroundings. In his work he swaggers and acts with a sense of false pride and confidence. This illustrates again the helmsman's detribalization, for, while performing a useful function he is, at the same time, "unstable." At the first "call of the wild," as when the steamboat is being attacked, he reverts back to primitive and irrational behavior. At this point, the helmsman belongs neither to the attacking natives, nor to the white men who command the boat. It is the result of such uncertainty of identity that the helmsman has degenerated, that he is killed. "Poor fool!" says Marlow ". . . he had no restraint, no restraint—just like Kurtz—a tree swayed by the wind."

Yet, ambiguously, Marlow recognizes that while the helmsman lacked restraint, in his death he was reclaimed by the mysterious forces of the Dark Continent. He gripped the spear that killed him "like something precious, with an air of being afraid I would try to take it away from him." And finally, "as though in response to some sign we could not see, to some whisper we could not hear, he frowned heavily, and that frown gave to his black death mask an inconceivably sombre, brooding, and menacing expression."

Themes

The Theme of Restraint

The introduction to this study guide briefly explored Conrad's belief in fidelity. In a large part such fidelity can operate only through the medium of restraint and the importance of restraint is stressed throughout *Heart of Darkness*. This theme expounds Conrad's philosophy that through devotion to duty man can discharge his obligation to society. In *Heart of Darkness*, Marlow is saved by restraint. Kurtz is doomed by the lack of it.

The theme of restraint is first introduced on the deck of the *Nellie*. The first narrator, who has been reflecting on the service done to the people who have lived on the banks of the Thames, concludes his thought with "What greatness had not floated on the ebb of that river . . . !" Marlow has different ideas, for the Thames also "has been one of the dark places of the earth." He imagines how the Romans felt upon first entering this then-savage land. Many of them must have perished doing their job but, they did it and did it well. What about the young Roman "coming out here . . . to mend his fortunes?" Marlow wonders. Marlow paints a picture of this young man beginning to "feel [that] the savagery, the utter savagery, had closed round him." He is worked on by "the fascination of the abomination. . . . Imagine the growing regrets . . . the surrender, the hate." Marlow adds that the Romans were interested in nothing but robbery and murder and says that "is very proper for those who tackle a darkness."

But Marlow says that, before he went to Africa, he held different conceptions about the colonization of the Congo because that colonization had "an idea at the back of it." Despite a vague uneasiness, he assumed that restraint would operate there. Then he reaches the Company station and receives his first rude shock. Everything there seems meaningless. He sees no evidence of that "devotion to efficiency" that makes the idea work. In the midst of this confusion, Marlow meets a "miracle." The chief accountant has the restraint that it takes to get the job done. In the depths of the jungle he keeps up his appearance and his books are in "apple-pie order." Marlow respects this fellow—he has backbone.

The manager is a disappointment. He is "a common trader" who lacks the restraint necessary for a white man's leadership. The manager allows his "boy" to treat the other whites with "provoking insolence," which can only undermine the European position. The idea implies that the white man is different; he is bringing his superior civilization to these "ignorant millions" and must rule as much by moral example as by force. The manager has betrayed his trust and through lack of restraint (or fidelity) has upset the balance between colonizer and native.

In contrast, the cannibals, some of those "ignorant millions," are almost totally characterized by restraint. They outnumber the whites "thirty to five" and could easily fill their starving bellies. Marlow "would have as soon expected restraint from a hyena prowling amongst the corpses of a battlefield." The cannibals' action is "one of those human secrets that baffle probability."

When Marlow finds the seaman's book in the reed hut, he is also baffled, and the reader shares this bafflement. What would a manual belonging to a master in His Majesty's navy be doing in the heart of Africa? Although it is not an exciting volume, one can see that it has "a singleness of intention, an honest concern for the right way of going to work." The book is symbolic of the restraint, the fidelity, that binds the British seaman and the British Empire to a spirit of service—the spirit of service that Marlow finds so lacking in deepest Africa.

Kurtz is the essence of the lack of restraint Marlow sees everywhere. Kurtz has "kicked himself loose from the earth." He owes no allegiance to anything except those animal powers, those various lusts, those unpermitted aspirations lurking in the darkness of his inner station. Marlow also responds to these dark callings; indeed, he almost becomes their captive. He confuses the beat of the drum (the call to man's primitive side) with his own heartbeat, and is pleased. Yet, he does not slip over the edge as Kurtz does. Marlow keeps to the track. When he is confronted with the ultimate evil where a man "must fall back on [his] own innate strength, upon [his] own capacity for faithfulness," he is able to do so, he shows the necessary restraint.

The Theme of Isolation

In the beginning pages Marlow talks to a group of friends aboard the *Nellie*. Oddly enough, although he is part of the

114

group, he is, in one respect, isolated. Marlow sits cross-legged with the ascetic aspect of a Buddhalike idol. This description readies the reader for an account of Marlow's spiritual journey to inner space, which parallels his physical journey to the inner station. This journey to the center of one's self must be made in isolation, and is reflected in Marlow's external isolation as he nears the inner station.

Marlow's sense of apartness is introduced the moment he departs from Europe. Time passes slowly on the steamer, and he has no "point of contact" with the men aboard the French vessel. This feeling of isolation deepens as he leaves the sea. He is a man who knows the water, but is a stranger to the land and finds it dark, grim and forbidding. For Marlow, the trip to Africa and the trip up the river are "like a weary pilgrimage."

At the company station he meets and admires the chief accountant. But Marlow can never quite identify with this accountant who wrote and wrote and occasionally "stood up for exercise." At the central station, Marlow has even less reason to identify with the manager or the brickmaker because they represent everything Marlow detests. There is no honesty in either of them. In turn, they are alienated from Marlow because they think he has connections in Europe which he will use to their disadvantage.

As the steamer approaches Kurtz's station, Marlow's isolation is heightened. The pilgrims look positively un- wholesome to him and, in his hope that the cannibals will not consider him one of the pilgrims, he creates a further barrier between himself and the others. Marlow's isolation reaches the point of no return at the inner station. When he tells the manager that Kurtz is "a remarkable man," Marlow finds himself "lumped along with . . . a partisan of methods for which the time was not ripe. [He] was unsound." The pilgrims also look upon Marlow with disfavor and, after Kurtz dies, Marlow is completely cut off from the party aboard the steamer.

Such isolation will continue, as is evidenced by Marlow's posture on the deck of the *Nellie*. Except in rare cases—such as with the first narrator—Marlow's Congo experience has given him such tremendous insight that he cannot communicate with the majority of mankind. They do not understand, cannot understand, as they have not faced the darkness. Indeed, most of them are unaware that the darkness exists.

The Theme of Hollow Men

On December 6, 1902, Edward Garnett wrote a review of *Heart of Darkness* from which the following excerpt is taken:

> A most amazing, consummate piece of artistic diablerie—an analysis of the white man's morale when let loose from European restraint, and planted down in the tropics as an "emissary of light" armed to the teeth to make trade profits out of subject races.

There is no doubt that, among other things, the book is an indictment of colonial methods. Taken as such it mounts an attack on the quality of men who are most successful at the business of "taking it [the loot] away from those who have a different complexion or slightly flatter noses than ourselves." The method Conrad uses in his attack is the theme of hollow men. They may be common (the manager) or uncommon (Kurtz), but they all have something vital missing from their make-up. The manager is a man without entrails. The brickmaker is "a papier-mâché Mephistopheles" through whom Marlow feels he could poke a finger. And Kurtz—the most successful of ivory traders—is no more than a voice echoing from an empty shell.

To accept the theme of hollow men as an indictment of colonial methods, and nothing more, is inadequate. Although there is some disagreement on exactly what Conrad is saying through Kurtz and the manager, it seems reasonable to assume that their emptiness points toward Conrad's basic belief that fidelity is the average man's salvation. It is the way to be; the way to defeat the surrounding darkness.

116

Levels of Meaning

Initiation Level

This level is related to most other levels of meaning and synthesizes them to some extent.

For our purposes, initiation can be understood as the first existential ordeal, crisis or encounter with experience in the life of man. As a process, initiation leads to an authentic experience of "living" in the world. Its end is recognition and confirmation of the good and evil invested in existence. Thus, the process of initiation is the journey from innocence to experience. The idea of initiation derives from the story of Adam and the Fall. In *Heart of Darkness*, Marlow is recalling the period of his initiation from innocence to the world of experience. Before going to the Congo, Marlow was like Adam before the Fall. His psychological, moral and spiritual circumstance was prior to experience and, in this state, he was fundamentally innocent. He was a sailor unconditioned by social morality. He was alone but self-reliant and self-determining. When he decided to go to the Congo he was advancing hopefully into an unknown world, ready to encounter whatever awaited him with the assistance of the qualities inherent in his nature. In this world, Marlow confronts the various evils that man in his 'civilized' state in Europe would not consider possible. While the man in Europe lives in a state of illusion, Marlow comes face to face with the "heart of darkness," the reality of existence that lies at the heart of all life. Although European civilization sees itself as essentially good, Marlow discovers that man, the embodiment of this civilization, is essentially both evil and good.

Life has always been identified with knowledge, both in the story of Adam and in grail legends. The ordeal of the hero is the encounter with the knowledge of evil, and the reward of this knowledge is life.

That Marlow saw his adventure as the archetypal embodiment of the Adamic initiation is clear. The principal symbol, aside from the forest, is the river. The chief motif is Marlow's journey up the river, which "seemed to throw a kind of light on everything about me—and into my thoughts." Indeed, like Adam tempted by Satan in the shape of a snake, Marlow is "charmed" by the Congo River, which resembles a snake. Marlow finally confronts the incarnation of Satanic evil in Kurtz but, instead of rejecting Kurtz as the pilgrims do, Marlow realizes that the knowledge of Kurtz's evil is necessary in order to fully understand the value of the good qualities of restraint. Kurtz's evil ironically contains good, as Marlow recognizes. The knowledge of good and evil allows Marlow to become fully conscious of what it means to live: he gains redemption as an individual. When he returns to Europe, because of the knowledge and experience he acquired as a successful initiate, he is alienated, an outsider to society. At the end of the novel, Marlow is alone and separate from the others aboard the *Nellie*. He "sat apart, indistinct and silent, in a pose of a meditating Buddha."

Social, Economic and Satirical Level

Heart of Darkness has as its basis a true, historical account of European exploration and colonialism. During the latter part of the nineteenth century colonialism was reaching its peak. The center of interest for European colonial powers was Africa, specifically the region of the Congo basin. The Portuguese (the original pioneers), the British, the Dutch and the French were the chief nations competing for African territory, and their rivalry became so clamorous that, at one point, there was serious danger of war between them. This fever was stimulated by various successful explorations and proclamations of the time: the discoveries of Stanley and Rhodes, the personal ambition of Leopold II of Belgium who wanted "to open to civilization the only part of our globe where Christianity has not penetrated and to pierce the darkness which envelops the entire population."

Conrad, who had himself experienced at first hand the actual practices of colonialism, was aware that the noble and exalted intentions and the so-called humanitarian missions to Africa, were merely a facade to extract the bounty of ivory, diamonds and gold available there in fabulous quantities. The motive to civilize or, as Marlow's aunt says, to wean "those ignorant millions from their horrid ways" was the pretext to exploit the land for profit in the "vilest scramble for loot" the world has known. The difference—the discrepancy between what people believe exists and what, in reality, does exist takes the level of social satire in Conrad's *Heart of Darkness*.

Conrad's spokesman, Marlow, is the relatively detached

observer who transmits what he sees in an ironic tone which provokes satirical comment throughout the novel. His journey from Europe to Africa and back to Europe is an intentional pattern which enables the moral values of European culture to be exposed and satirized. Their worth is revealed when the exponents of these values are morally isolated from the confines of organized society. When Marlow returns, his illumination is the criterion whereby European culture is judged and condemned. What Marlow learns about these values in the Congo becomes the measure of the hypocrisy and false idealism of European civilization.

What Marlow discovered was that the white man who had come to Africa professing to bring progress and light to the darkest regions had himself been deprived of the sanctions of his European social order. He had also been alienated from the old established ways. Having to rely upon his own inner, spiritual resources, he is revealed as weak and, as a result, he is damned by his greed, his sloth, his hypocrisy and brutality. He may be so corrupted by his absolute power over the natives, like Kurtz is, that he creates his own terrifying hell.

The behavior of the white man in Africa becomes worse than the cannibalism of the black man. The latter adheres to an aboriginal existence which is natural to him. The European, on the other hand, unable to identify with the African environment and lacking the kind of individuality that defines Marlow, becomes a hollow man, empty of humanity, hence, unnaturally savage.

Most of the white men Marlow meets are satirized. The brickmaker at the central station makes no bricks. The pilgrims, those "greedy phantoms," seem to do nothing but plot and intrigue. The manager has "no genius for organizing, for initiative, for order even." The devoted band of the Eldorado Exploring Expedition, led by the manager's uncle has "not an atom of foresight or of serious intention in the whole batch . . . and . . . did not seem aware these things are wanted for the work of the world."

Instead of exemplifying the progress and light of their civilization, the actions of the white men, according to Marlow, have "the touch of insanity" about them. Rather than construct they destroy, but their ruinous conduct is made to appear even more absurd because they engage in blind destruction.

The Level of Quest

On the simple, narrative level, *Heart of Darkness* is a story of a man's adventure. To make this kind of tale entertaining Conrad has used the ingredients that make adventure all the more appealing—danger, mystery, suspense, escape, exotic background, plots and intrigues and unexpected attack. Marlow's journey is an obstacle course and the obstacles are not only physical. Besides snags in the river and dense jungle, he must keep his eye open for cannibals and the machinations of various Company agents.

However, Conrad's purpose is not merely to entertain, but also to instruct. As a result, the trappings of the conventional adventure tale become the vehicle of something more important. Simply, on this level the tale can be seen as a grail quest. The metaphor of the quest ("a weary pilgrimage amongst hints for nightmares") derives from the Middle Ages when knights believed that Christ's chalice still existed. Many of them went on journeys in search of the Holy Grail in the belief that he who found and could see the grail received an illumination.

The level of quest in *Heart of Darkness* is most apparent in the structure of the action. Marlow, as the central figure, is like a knight seeking the grail and his journey follows the archetype. His many references to the unknown and secret places of the earth, the farthest point of navigation in the Dark Continent, his sudden realization that he is not going to "the centre of a continent" but to "the centre of the earth"—these assertions made *prior* to the voyage establish the setting of a quest. The journey itself is an ordeal. The river, the jungle, the sunken steamship and the torturous forest paths are all appropriate obstacles. At the central station he is given a routine task of going up the river to retrieve a sick Company agent. Little by little, Marlow learns about Kurtz. As Marlow's interest in him increases, so do the hazards that separate him from Kurtz. Finally, near the end, Marlow comes to realize that Kurtz is the "object" of his quest.

In contrast to Marlow, the pilgrims do not seek the enlightenment to be gained from a spiritual journey. Their goal is ivory; the "vilest scramble for loot." The idea that the greedy traders are faithless pilgrims, is made explicit when, instead of the voices of angels, ". . . the word 'ivory' rang in the air, was whispered, was sighed—you would think they were praying for it." Further, as those aboard the steamship approach Kurtz's sanctuary, "The word ivory would ring in the air for a while . . . into the silence. . . ." Their ignobility and avarice are in ironic contrast to the noble restraint of Marlow. Indeed, his restraint is the armor that protects him from the greed, malice and envy of his companions. They have no armor, and their staves are like crutches that support their hollowness.

The grail motif is associated with the light-dark symbolism prevalent throughout the novel. The grail is light and it gives illumination to those who can see it. This is the light that Marlow seeks in the heart of darkness. Paradoxically, the light of the grail he finds, intensifies darkness. However, Marlow is illuminated: "It threw a kind of light on everything about me." For the manager and the other faithless pilgrims, there can be no illumination. Nonetheless, the illumination for Marlow is as unspeakable as it is profound. As a consequence, the meaning of the tale can only be conveyed obliquely like the "glow that brings out the haze."

Mythological Level

In *Heart of Darkness*, Conrad is not only describing a psychological experience, he is dealing with a significant moral conflict. He is depicting Marlow's discovery of evil and the responsibilities to himself and to others which this knowledge places upon him. In telling the story of Marlow's attainment of this knowledge, Conrad has employed the imagery and symbolism reminiscent of the traditional voyage into Hades. By relating Marlow's journey to the descent into hell, Conrad is able to show the latent world of the inner self. Through image and symbol, he evokes the classical voyage of the mythic hero who explores the underworld to discover some piece of information that is important to him. In doing so, he reveals the depths of his own and his nation's conscience.

Marlow's pattern of descent into hell parallels, to some extent, heroic journeys described in Homer's *Odyssey*, Vergil's *Aeneid*, and Dante's *Inferno*. For example, Aeneas' descent in the *Aeneid* is an initiation for the role of leader of the Roman people. For Vergil, as for Conrad, truth is to be found in darkness and thus Aeneas' journey to hell is one way by which he discovers the tragedy inherent in the public world, as well as the price Rome's imperial power must pay for its shortcomings.

121

Like Aeneas, Marlow comes to understand himself, his moral responsibilities, and the tragic limitations involved in human freedom, through not only a study of the mysteries of his own mind but, also, through the discovery of social injustices.

Kurtz, on the other hand, starting out like Marlow as an "emissary of light," cannot conquer the potential for evil within himself. Marlow learns through Kurtz's experience that a man is defined by his work. Kurtz's work has created a jungle hell which destroys him. His final message, "The horror! The horror!"—information from hell—ironically becomes a judgment on the morality of society.

The traditional imagery and symbolism employed for Marlow's journey through hell and his meeting with its arch-inhabitant, Kurtz, is cleary apparent. From the start, Marlow is fated by the need of his own soul to conquer the darkness within. Africa itself represents hell and the Congo symbolizes the river Styx, the river that separates the world of the living from the world of the dead in classical mythology.

The more Marlow penetrates this hell, the more sin and damnation become apparent. At the first station is the accountant, doomed by an incapacity for suffering, in limbo; at the next are the ivory traders, immersed in their own greed and corruption. Finally, at the center of the underworld is Kurtz, a living Lucifer, taking on the attributes of all the sins in which he had participated. Throughout, the description of the jungle, the dense white fog on the river, the unseen natives, the shrunken heads mounted on posts before Kurtz's hut, give the land a hellish atmosphere.

Poetic Level

In a famous letter, Conrad remarks that to write a story "you must cultivate your poetic faculty . . . you must search the darkest corners of your heart . . . for the image."

The very title itself suggests the symbolic and the poetic imagery of the novel, which may, in a very important sense, be regarded as a poem. The title, *Heart of Darkness*, contains in its range of symbolic significance the "sinister resonance" of the entire story.

It is certain that Conrad meant his story to be read as symbolic poetry. Ford Madox Ford, Conrad's friend and collaborator, said that Conrad was experimenting with blank verse during the late 1890s and used it in *Heart of Darkness*. The student has only to scan the lines to realize that Conrad's prose falls into verse rhythm, with the influences of Biblical prose and Shakespearean verse being evident. For instance:

> The sun/ set;/ the dusk/ fell on the/ stream,
> And lights/ began/ to appear/ along the/ shore/

—obviously the familiar iambic pentameter. Again:

> Going/ up that/ river/ was like/ travelling
> Back to the/ earliest/ beginn/ings of the/ world.

Characters are symbolic rather than literal. One has only to think of the knitting women as the Fates; or the pilgrims—the hollow men, or Kurtz himself as a vague, shadowy embodiment of evil to appreciate the powerfully poetic quality of the characterization. Compare *Heart of Darkness* with Dante's *Inferno* or Vergil's *Aeneid*, two epic poems, for corroboration of the poetic reading of Conrad's story as far as character and incident are concerned.

The poetic level may be most apparent when one examines the many and diverse images. It is not so much through the poetic prose rhythms, nor even the almost allegorical characterization that Conrad achieves the poetic level. Rather it is through Conrad's presentation of the theme of moral irresponsibility in a modern wasteland and through the use of images that theme. In *Heart of Darkness* some of the main imagery has to do with death, decay, futility, and metallic substances which are antagonistic to human manipulation and with rusting moribund machinery.

At the beginning of the novella, a sombre imagery is established in the description of the Thames in Roman times— the Congo of its day—with its "cold, fog, tempests, disease, exile, death." In Brussels, at the Company office, Marlow encounters a "whited sepulchre" and two guardians of hell knitting the fate of his trip. Futility and heartlessness reside in the images of the journey: the sterile landing of the soldiers; the farcical names of places they visit; the gunboat's futile and incomprehensible shelling of the shore; the hanged Swede; the wasted houses; the rusting boiler; the railway truck lying on its back; the dying savages; the wasted shades in this hell; the heartlessly correct accountant with everything in "apple-pie order" while death is all around him; the cunning, heartless manager and his pilgrims—men stuffed with straw; the nightmare journey to the inner station; Kurtz with his "ivory" head—turned into the material of his corruption; the "unspeakable rites" of his degradation; his mistress—an embodiment of the jungle itself; the white fog; the battle with the natives who only resist the invasion of their mysterious privacy; the death of the helmsman—and more.

Only a brief examination of Conrad's use of poetic words, imagery, symbol and characterization should suffice to indicate the power, depth and beauty of Conrad's concept of his theme, which is apparent on many levels of understanding. And here may be its deepest and universal appeal—*Heart of Darkness* is a poem, a symbolic conception of great suggestive power, significant depth and inexpressible beauty.

Symbolism and Style

Light and dark symbolism is found throughout the story. In sharper contrast, black and white play an important part in *Heart of Darkness*. The values attached to the two are not consistent. At times, white symbolizes civilization and black, savagery. In other passages, evil is broadly revealed in the white man and the blacks represent higher values. Conrad's technique is focussed on contrasts, parallels and comparisons. Sometimes, these are overtly presented; at other times, it is up to the reader to detect implications.

Black is the dominant image. The two women in the Company headquarters in Brussels knit black wool. The two hens in the Congo, over which an argument leads to the death of Marlow's predecessor, are black. The deserted hut has holes in its roof that "gaped black from afar." There are "shiny patches on the black creek." Describing Kurtz's station house, Marlow sees wooden knobs on the fence posts that, on closer inspection are revealed to be "black . . . sunken skulls." The jungle, when seen from the boat, is "so dark green as to be almost black."

Another characteristic device used by Conrad, which contributes a certain tension to the novella, is the use of controlled counterpoint to link otherwise parallel or similar images. The civilized setting of the Thames as against the primitive Congo is one example. Kurtz's overt evil and the covert evil of the manager is another. The native woman symbolizes primitive, physical passion, and Kurtz's pale Intended stands for European spiritual values. Yet, both women share an interest in Kurtz that points to a harmonic interweaving of their respect for the man. The darkness of Africa is contrasted against the "whited sepulchre" of the graveyardlike modern city of Brussels.

Much of what has been said pertains to style as well as to symbolism and other characteristics of Conrad's writing. What is style? Conrad himself wrote that, "the whole truth lies in the presentation; therefore the expression should be studied in the interest of veracity. This is the only morality of art apart from subject." Hence, the "how" of storytelling is part of the "what" of the story. Each writer has his own distinctive manner. Conrad's style is rooted in his imagery, his symbolic presentation, his figures of speech, his contrasting, comparing and parallelling techniques. A remarkably rich vocabulary and the cumulative use of powerful adjectives suggesting atmosphere are among the stylistic features of Conrad's writing.

Although Conrad is generally recognized as a master of English prose, there is one objection to his style: the tendency of trying to express ideas that can hardly be communicated in words (e.g., "impalpable greyness," "invisible wilderness," "inaccessible distance," "unextinguishable regrets," etc.). However, the rhythmic, harmonious motion of Conrad's words lends itself to scanning. This musical quality, enhanced by the use of alliteration, makes Conrad's writing poetic.

Selected Criticisms

.... For the art of 'Heart of Darkness'—as in every psychological masterpiece—lies in the relation of the things of the spirit to the things of the flesh, of the invisible life to the visible, of the sub-conscious life within us, our obscure motives and instincts, to our conscious actions, feelings and outlook. Just as landscape art implies the artist catching the exact relation of a tree to the earth from which it springs, and of the earth to the sky, so the art of 'Heart of Darkness' implies the catching of infinite shades of the white man's uneasy, disconcerted, and fantastic relations with the exploited barbarism of Africa; it implies the acutest analysis of the deterioration of the white man's *morale*, when he is let loose from European restraint, and planted down in the tropics as an 'emissary of light' armed to the teeth, to make trade profits out of the 'subject races.' The weirdness, the brilliance, the psychological truth of this masterly analysis of two Continents in conflict, of the abysmal gulf between the white man's system and the black man's comprehension of its results, is conveyed in a rapidly rushing narrative which calls for close attention on the reader's part. But the attention once surrendered, the pages of the narrative are as enthralling as the pages of Dostoevsky's *Crime and Punishment*. The stillness of the sombre African forests, the glare of sunshine, the feeling of dawn, of noon, of night on the tropical rivers, the isolation of the unnerved, degenerating whites staring all day and every day at the Heart of Darkness which is alike meaningless and threatening to their own creed and conceptions of life, the helpless bewilderment of the unhappy savages in the grasp of their flabby and rapacious conquerors—all this is a page torn from the life of the Dark Continent—a page which has been hitherto carefully blurred and kept away from European eyes. There is no 'intention' in the story, no *parti pris*, no prejudice one way or the other; it is simply a piece of art, fascinating and remorseless, and the artist is but intent on presenting his sensations in that sequence and arrangement whereby the meaning or the meaninglessness of the white man in uncivilised Africa can be felt in its really significant aspects. If the story is too strong meat for the ordinary reader, let him turn to 'Youth,' wherein the song of every man's youth is indeed sung.

Edward Garnett. *Academy and Literature*, Dec. 6, 1902.

Kurtz is a personal embodiment, a dramatization, of all that Conrad felt of futility, degradation, and horror in what the Europeans in the Congo called "progress," which meant the exploitation of the natives by every variety of cruelty and treachery known to greedy man. Kurtz was to Marlow, penetrating this country, a name, constantly recurring in people's talk, for cleverness and enterprise. . . . The blackness and mystery of his character tone in with the savage mystery of the Congo, and they develop *pari passu* with the atmosphere of shadowy horror. This development is conducted cumulatively by insensitive degrees, by carefully correlated news items, new intimations; and all this process is controlled through the consciousness of Marlow. Thus we have a triumph of atmospheric effect produced with the technique of the limited point of view, a story in a class with "The Fall of the House of Usher" and "The Turn of the Screw."

Joseph Warren Beach. *The Twentieth Century Novel*, Appleton Century, 1932.

In Conrad's presentation of a modern world in which material image is one with human image, we have a symbolic re-creation that is particularly relevant to the twentieth century. This story, with its aversion to the amoral acquisitive spirit and with its dramatization of the horrors inherent in the loss of responsibility, closes out the nineteenth century with a resounding shriek of moral disapproval. Even though Kurtz at the moment of death recognizes the infinite horrors of his inhumanity, his moral victory is no easy remedy for what he had perpetrated. And even though Marlow's journey up the Congo ends in his returning with a repentant devil, the memory of this redeemed soul must be preserved by a lie. Conrad's political prescience of modern propaganda methods was never more powerful. All that remained to the spiritually exhausted Marlow was the faith of Kurtz's fiancée, rooted as she was not in reality but in illusions; and yet, ironically, her faith remained the only light under a sky "that seemed to lead into the heart of an immense darkness."

Frederick R. Karl. *A Reader's Guide to Joseph Conrad*, Noonday Press, 1960.

All the concerns of men in Europe seemed to Marlowe to be petty and niggardly, of no account, after he had witnessed the denouement of Kurtz's great struggle with the masses of black men in Africa. Kurtz had failed—his only victory had been in

128

that he had retained enough presence of mind to name what he had found in himself there "the horror—the horror." But that failure had been a greater success than any that Marlowe could conceive of any one's having in Europe. Why did not Marlowe go back to Africa and take up Kurtz's life there as Stanley had taken up Livingston's? The answer is simply that he knew he wasn't man enough. It was his pusillanimity that had motivated his successful struggle to rescue Kurtz from throwing in his lot with the savages.

However, Marlowe knew where his heart was, even if his bodily courage was not stout enough to follow it. He had seen a god in action, and he had heard his voice. Kurtz had had a voice like a god's and its tones were to remain louder in Marlowe's ears than anything that was to sound in them thereafter. And behind Kurtz's voice, for Marlowe, is the voice of those millions of irrational savages, all that life which will continue on whether or not Marlowe goes back to watch it. The savages partake of Kurtz's greatness, because they were able, willing, and eager to recognize it and to do obeisance where obeisance was due; while the white employees of the company are base and contemptible jackals, mere ivory-snatchers for the Home Office.

What we have here is obviously a rejection of two groups by Kurtz, and a lukewarm, mitigated, acceptance of one group by Marlowe. However, it is not a deficiency but rather an excess in group-feeling that brings about these total and partial rejections. Both Kurtz and Marlowe are drawn to two incompatible groups, and the savage group is fundamentally incompatible to both men because it is, culturally, so many centuries far back in past time that to commingle with it made Kurtz feel as though his very soul were decomposing within him. Kurtz could not go back that far, and Marlowe much less; but the attempt to do so on Kurtz's part, and the temptation to do so on Marlowe's, destroyed Kurtz's and nearly destroyed Marlowe's ability and desire to regain a place in their natal group. Kurtz strayed so far from his natal group that he could not get back to it, and Marlowe's distance from his group became so great that its gravitational pull on him became faint almost to extinction. The indirectly expressed assumption of the two men's experience is simply that, no matter how disillusioned the individual has become with the motivating values subscribed to by his group, he dies if he permits himself to become totally separated from that group. Both Kurtz and Marlowe sat in judgment on the society from which they sprang, but Kurtz died because he condemned and rejected that society while Marlowe lived because the loss of his esteem for his group did not prevent him from working out a modus vivendi that kept open at least some of the channels of communication between himself and the group to which he belonged.

Osborn Andreas. *Joseph Conrad, A Study in Non-conformity*, Archon Books, 1969 .

Since Marlow's narrative is a tale devoted primarily to a journey to the mysterious dark continent (the literal heart of darkness, Africa), a superficial view of the tale is simply that it is essentially an elaborate story involving confrontation with exotic natives, treacherous dangers of the jungle, brutal savagery, and even cannibalism. But such a view ignores larger meanings with which the work is implicitly concerned: namely, social and cultural implications; psychological workings of the cultivated European left to the uncivilized wilderness; and the richly colored fabric of symbolism that emerges slowly but inevitably from beneath the surface.

Heart of Darkness can also be examined for its social and cultural commentaries. It is fairly obvious that a perverted version of the "White Man's Burden" was the philosophy adopted by the ivory hunters at the Inner Station. Kurtz's "Exterminate the brutes!" shows the way a white man can exploit the helpless savage. The futile shelling from the gunboat into the jungle is also vividly portrayed as a useless, brutal, and absurd act perpetrated against a weaker, more uncivilized culture than the one that nurtured Kurtz. . . .

Heart of Darkness is one of literature's most sombre fictions. It explores the fundamental questions about man's nature: his capacity for evil; the necessity for restraint; the effect of physical darkness and isolation on a civilized soul; and the necessity of relinquishing pride for one's own spiritual salvation. E. M. Forster's censure of Conrad may be correct in many ways, but it refuses to admit that through such philosophical ruminations Conrad has allowed generations of readers to ponder humanity's own heart of darkness.

Wayne E. Haskin. *1,300 Critical Evaluations of Selected Novels and Plays* (Edited by F.N. Magill), Salem Press, 1978.

One of the major assumptions on which 'Heart of Darkness' rests is that if we want to find out the 'real' truth about man—what his 'essential' nature is—we must inquire into his origins. This basically evolutionary view holds that civilization is something merely imposed on man's essential nature—that culture does not eradicate, but merely keeps in check, his primitive instincts. In this sense, Marlow's journey to the Inner Station—to the heart of the African darkness—is a voyage into his ancestral past; and what Kurtz in the end discovers for himself is what Marlow has already grasped: that the ideals of European life form no part of man's essential self—that the heart of the European citizen, for all the endeavours of his education, remains an abode of darkness. But this is only part of Kurtz's meaning. The rest is that this truth is a terrible one—that is to say, that the values it denies survive the denial, in the sense that they remain supremely important. According to this view, teleological rather than evolutionary, the 'real' truth about man is not merely where he comes from, but where he is going to; his 'essential' nature is not found merely by uncovering his past but also by defining his future. Thus civilization cannot be dismissed, as it were, as a defective actuality: it should more properly be regarded as a potential to be sustained, or a destination to be pursued. The criterion for reality is no longer existence, but possibility. Man's goals do not have to be realized in order to be made 'real': it is enough that they be taken seriously. That Kurtz's last cry should not have been 'a word of careless contempt' is, as Marlow emphasizes, a fact of supreme importance to him, for it proves that Kurtz—and again in this like Marlow before him—has felt the need, in the face of what he has at last recognized as darkness, for an alternative reality.

Jacques Berthoud. *Joseph Conrad, The Major Phase*, Cambridge University Press, 1978.

Suggested Study Topics

1. What constitutes the idea of utopia in *Heart of Darkness*?
2. While Conrad exposes the corruption, destruction and evil of the white man in Africa, does he present any ideal from which this degradation can be judged?
3. What are the consequences of moral isolation in *Heart of Darkness*?
4. In what way do the native woman and the Intended symbolize two different ways of life?
5. In what way does the evil (hollowness) of Kurtz differ from the evil (hollowness) of the Company agents?
6. In what way does Conrad satirize civilization? How civilized is man?
7. Characterize the manager.
8. We usually associate black with evil and white with good; to what extent has Conrad reversed this?
9. Discuss Conrad's use of irony. Describe at least three instances of irony.
10. What is the meaning of "the horror! the horror!"?
11. How many choices does Marlow make? Why must he choose? What are the consequences of his final choice?
12. Using at least three major symbols, discuss the symbolism in *Heart of Darkness*.

Bibliography

Baines, Jocelyn. *Joseph Conrad, A Critical Biography*. New York: McGraw Hill, 1960.

Beebe, Maurice. "Criticism of Joseph Conrad: A Selected Checklist with an Index to Studies of Separate Works," *Modern Fiction Studies*, 1, No. 1 (Feb. 1955).

Bruffee, D.A. "Lesser Nightmare: Marlow's Lie in *Heart of Darkness*," *Modern Language Quarterly*, XXV (Sept. 1964).

Bruss, Paul. *Conrad's Early Sea Fiction*. Lewisburg, Pa.: Bucknell University Press, 1979.

Ford, Ford Madox. *Joseph Conrad: A Personal Remembrance*. Boston: Little, Brown & Co., 1924.

Gordon, John A. *Joseph Conrad: The Making of a Novelist*. Cambridge: Harvard University Press, 1941.

Guerard, Albert, Jr. *Conrad the Novelist*. Cambridge: Harvard University Press, 1958.

Harkness, Bruce, ed. *Conrad's Heart of Darkness and the Critics*. Belmont, Ca.: Wadsworth Pub. Co., 1960.

Kimborough, Robert, ed. *Joseph Conrad: Heart of Darkness*. (text, background, sources and criticism) New York: Norton Critical Editions, 1963.

Leavis, F.R. *The Great Tradition*. Garden City, New York: Doubleday Anchor Books, 1954.

Moser, Thomas. *Joseph Conrad: Achievement and Decline*. Cambridge: Harvard University Press, 1957.

Mudrick, Marvin, ed. *Conrad: A Collection of Critical Essays*. Englewood Cliffs, N.J.: Prentice Hall, 1966.

Newhouse, Neville. *Joseph Conrad*. New York: Arco, 1969.

Stallman, R.W., ed. *The Art of Joseph Conrad, A Critical Symposium*. Ann Arbor: Michigan State University Press, 1960.

Wright, Walter F. *Joseph Conrad on Fiction*. Lincoln: University of Nebraska Press, 1949.

_____. *Romance and Tragedy in Joseph Conrad*. Lincoln: University of Nebraska Press, 1949.

NOTES

NOTES

NOTES

NOTES

NOTES